T0365347

GOTMOL
GRACING OUR TIME'S MEANING OF LIFE
BELONGSONGS OF THE HOLD'S COVENANTAL HOLDINGS

If we could sing but one glorious song,
We'd throat a choral symphony to life,
With every movement's refrain, loud and strong,
Sounding melodies transcendent of strife.
A love song more real than we could but dream,
Crescendoed through each word and instrument,
As leaves sing winds and rocks the splashing stream,
As wolves howl and loam batons enchantment.
We would not forget our blood's violence,
How the mortal tympanum is beaten,
Yet the strings will out-play the swill of chance,
The horns blare harmonies that won't weaken.
As life hurts, yet glows in a glory shroud,
Our song will rise-up and be cried aloud.

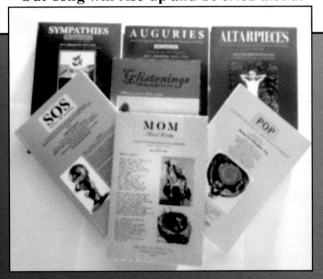

Michael D. O'Kelly, Poet
'Apo'kstrophes'
AFIRADAPO
A Fireflies At Dawn Poiesis
2021

To order additional copies of this book, contact:
Xlibris
844-714-8691
www.Xlibris.com
Orders@Xlibris.com

ISBN: Softcover   978-1-6641-5411-7
           EBook   978-1-6641-5412-4

Library of Congress Control Number: 2021901404

Print information available on the last page

Rev. date: 03/30/2021

GOTMOL

GRACING OUR TIME'S MEANING OF LIFE
BELONGSONGS OF THE HOLD'S COVENANTAL HOLDINGS

A BOOK OF POETRY-PHILOSOPHY
AND SPIRITUALITY
With The Help of Science
The Seventh Sense of The Hold
&
Glistenings From The Dawn's Balm on the Lawn

by

Michael D. O'Kelly, Poet
'Apo'kstrophes"

AFIRADAPO
A Fireflies At Dawn Poiesis
2021

GRACENOTES THAT HOLD

"let the sunshine, let the sunshine in, the sunshine in!" – *Aquarius*
"Now cracks a noble heart. Good Night, sweet prince.
And flights of angels sing thee to thy rest."
Horatio's words to Shakespeare's dying Hamlet.

"FLUCTUAT NEC MERGITUR"
Ancient Paris Slogan – "She is tossed by the waves, but does not sink."
This time – Notre Dame in Flames, her choir's not consumed.

"MUSIC OF THE SPHERES"
From Pythagoras to Plato to Boethius to Newton to --- String Theory!

"In vain does the God of War growl, snarl, roar, and try to interrupt with bombards, trumpets, and his whole tarantantaran . . . . Let us despise the barbaric neighings which echo through these noble lands and awaken our understanding and longing for the harmonies." Johannes Kepler in 1620.

"The arch never sleeps. Living in unison it holds. So long as each piece
does its work the arch is alive, singing, a restless choral."
Carl Sandburg

"I am that final thing - A man learning to sing."
Theodore Roethke

A work of art is determined by its manifesting
"une harmonie d'ensemble" – Matisse

"One touch of nature makes the whole world kin."
Shakespeare – *Troilus and Cressida*

"A-UM MANI PADME HUM"
Hindu Chant of "Behold! The jewel in the lotus!" O! Hear! Dualisms United as One!
Between Inhalation (Male) and Exhalation (Female) the Hold of Life.
The Primal Sound's Alive Through Humanity's Song!

BENNACHT! Gaelic Blessing!
LET THERE BE LIGHT! AND THERE WAS LIGHT! -- Genesis

"Again, wakes a noble heart. Another Day Dawns Sentient One!"
[AG-WA-A-NO-HE A-DA-DA-SE-ON]
"Hold True Sunshine! And choirs of Gracings sing your song aloud."
Of this Gracenotes & Belongsong as Choired in GOTMOL's
The Hold. – "That makes the whole world kin."

OF TENUTO AND FERMATA

FOUR MUSICAL NOTATIONS OF *H O L D I N G S*
AROUND ANY GRACENOTE AS VARIOUSLY HELD
TO ADVANCE THE MUSIC'S THEME AND BELONGSONG
One could consider this book as an "enchoiring elixir" of gracenotes around THE HOLD.

FROM *SYMPATHIES*

Alas, we never know how many
Songs we'll sing till there aren't any.
"Till The End of Time, Long As Stars Are In The Blue,
Long As There's A Spring, A Bird To Sing – I'll Go On Loving You."
We say "skoal" as we drink from the Grail,
. . . .to Love's victory o'er vicissitude! . . .
Donizetti's *L'eslisir d'amore* (Opera's first with aria duets) . . .
Had lovers drink a presumed elixir,
It's hope carrying each to reveal their love.
First to Nemorino who sings *Una Furtiva Lagrima* –

> *"A single secret tear…*
> *For just an instant the beating*
> *of her beautiful heart I could feel…*
> *to merge my sighs with hers…*
> *I could ask for nothing more, nothing more.*
> *Yes, I could die! Yes, I could die for love.*
> *(Si, puo morire! Si puo morir d'amor.)*

Oh, such epiphany and sympathy!
Such need for chemistry and alchemy!
Oh, needly elixirs of prophesy!

BEHOLD THE HOLD

DEDICATION

This GOTMOL is dedicated to my artist wife, Marilyn. I, and our three children, have been without her since 05/25/09. She still graces our everyday – both in memory, art and presence. She is very present in family gatherings, where we continue to flourish her ashes into the fire – thus to ceremoniously enliven her blaze and glow again. She was a Libra in sign, which is why I published her memorial book GLISTENINGS with Xlibris in 2010 – and have continued so with this and the three previous collections of 2020 – MOM-POP-SOS. Many poetries in each from her inspiration-memory. She was 65 when I took this "Staring" Reach of Apple-Picking photo of her. O! Balms of Dawn on the Lawn! O! Her Caressing Gracings of My Time's Meaning of Life!

REACHING FOR THE STARS

"The universe -- being composed of an enormous number of…vibrating strings – is akin to *a cosmic symphony.*"(p.146) "At this state, then, we should 'grab hold' of a string and 'pluck' it in all sorts of ways to determine the possible resonant patterns of vibration." (p.147) "Briefly put, the equations of string theory are so complicated that no one knows their exact form. . . . . Rather than having five distinct string theories, physicists are now convinced that there is *one* theory that sews all five into a unique . . .union . . .providing a powerful new vantage point for understanding the universe. . . .(p. 285) "And as our generation marvels at one new view of the universe -- our new way of asserting the world's coherence—we are fulfilling our part, contributing our rung to the human ladder *reaching for the stars.* (p. 387) (Brian Greene "The Elegant Universe" (Norton 1999).) -- Yes! Stars & Apples kin-akin to.

And One Elegant Maryl! Now Behold THE HOLD: Apples, Stars, and such as She!

So it is with GOTMOL -- The Lift – The Gift- The With – of Such EARTHANGELS – With Us Still.

GOTMOL'S PREFACING "HOLD" & "THE ANTHROPIC PRINCIPLE"

I knew if I kept looking I'd find a "physicists-philosopher" statement to assist this "poetic endeavor" of mine as it attempted to include their world. First of all, there was this brief explanation by Steven Weinberg in his THE FIRST THREE MINUTES, Basic Books, 1993: "This idea --- that the constants of nature must take values that allow for the existence of life and intelligence--- is known as the *anthropic principle*." (p. 187) There are weak and strong variations of this and the Wikipedia article is excellent for deeper penetration. It included this "weak" view quote from Rogen Penrose's THE EMPEROR'S NEW MIND, Chapter 10, wherein I've italicized the word HOLD as it appears:

"The argument can be used to explain why the conditions happen to be just right for the existence of (intelligent) life on Earth at the present time. For if it were not just right, then we should not have found ourselves to be here now, but somewhere else at some other appropriate time . . . . The issue ('puzzling physicists') concerned various striking numerical relations that are observed TO HOLD between the physical constants (*the gravitational constant, the mass of the proton, the age of the universe, etc.*). A puzzling aspect of this was that some of the relations HOLD only at the present epoch in the Earth's history, so we appear, coincidentally, to be living at a very special time (give or take a few million years!) This was later explained --- by the fact that this epoch coincided with the lifeline of what are called *main-sequence stars*, such as the Sun. At any other epoch, the argument ran, there would be no intelligent life around to measure the physical constants in question. --- So the coincidence had TO HOLD simply because there would be no intelligent life around only at the particular time that the coincidences DID HOLD."

Integral to this GOTMOL is the concept of THE HOLD, which gets various treatments throughout. I'm ever expressing from this anthropic platform of THE HOLD, which is a pervasive "constant" (even in randomness) that unites its function in the universe with that of THE HOLD of human consciousness and all the species. Our Hold is attuned/synced to that of the universe …somehow. We are epochally existent in this MAIN-SEQUENCE STAR/Solar-System-Hold of rotating/spinning planets maintaining their position. And Earth – holding-its-own within the holding constants of the known and unknown. -- In an ultimate sense, this HOLD, so operative throughout, is the "truest" existential clue to our meaning of life. Without it we could not put 2 & 2 together so that it holds in our consciousness and mental capacity to "grasp" such as E=mc2. And so it is that we know where life caresses/prospers and where it breaks-apart. The more we grasp what holds to hold us and we advance our meaning of being held – the more we grasp/get what Graces Our Time's *Meaning Of Life*. O! To be Initiated into the *Mysteries of Life*! Welcome to that other version of MOM – the *Magics of Meaning*. Hopefully, this GOTMOL will clarify the picture and expand your vision. It has mine. I'm increasingly moved to surmise the purpose of existence is THE HOLD: therefore, the same for us. It Sings Sound! Serves Whole! Feels Good! Holds Fast! Rings True. Holy Grail! Earthy Trail! Structures of ladders to climb higher.

O! The Reverberant Grace of it All!

[Yes, the Seventh Sense of The Hold. The five of sight, taste, touch, sound, smell have a sixth which is that big "I" of intuition/inspiration/intelligence. The 7th Sense percieves(lives with) – by virtue of the holistic interplay of these six – an existential reality of being held, holding-on, and being the creator of "holding patterns" that structure and define life as we know it. Namely, finding-framing-following the patterns/forms that "hold things together" – like trees, Toyotas, trinities: stars and species. Concepts of deity, transcendence, gods as absolutes which hold us as the held – come from this holistic sense of THE HOLD – in us and in all the holds of existence. The fact that the number 7 is the keystone-prime (chakaras all) between primes of 3/5 and 9/11 – strengthens its play of the day or week. Amazing to find seven orifices in the head: eyes/nostrils/mouth/ears. *O! Recall the Seven Breath Sounds of the Quintetoion. (see Glossary)]*

CONTENTS

IMAGES

Such poetries, breathings, and little dogs
Such images from thoughtful living
Are grateful gracings at any time's
Grasp for the meaning of life.

SECOND DEDICATION -- PROLOGUE

I'm, also, dedicating this GOTMOL to all the people I still see in my mind's eye, who have died and left me to keep the belongsong singing. Friends, colleagues, family, associates for this and that, celebrants for this and that: all thrived as gracenotes into the larger symphony still playing. Should add my dogs, too: Sank-Peg-Tania-Gulliver-Buber- Lance- Barney-Camp-DaisyDew. The parrot Sam and parakeet Tweetie. Now – a live cat -- Gertie. Too many people to name, but I've named the pets because they are symbolic of gracenotes to our own belongsong. I think most can relate to that. All persons experience this and all will have many persons in their mind's eye and personal symphonies.

Ahh! The Mind's Eye: the ME! More than memory – this is the every moment interplay of observer and observed. MEaWE! Worldly Embrace! AWEAEWA!

Behold those AUGURAL WISDOM ENERGIES of LOL – Life of Love/Love of Life, DeathInLife/ LifeInDeath. Add 'em up! Dawn to Dark/Dark to Dawn!

AWEAEWA-LOLALOL-LIDADIL-PAPAPAP
PredationAugursProcreation/ProcreationAugursPredation.
Both Portend the Prosperoion

And so it is that the pendulum swings back and forth in the process of existence. I've made it clear, from my ME-WE, that no philosophy of life and human destiny can be taken seriously if it does not begin with PREDATION/PREY. The Predatory/Prey Instinct (beyond Freud's Death Instinct and a major archetype Jung seems to have missed.) is in reciprocal alignment with the Procreation Instinct. This reciprocating PAP is the primal 'STRUCTURE" embedded in all of life and therefore – in us. The GOTMOL of any time is to thrive for life transcendent of predation being half the weight-wisdom of Being. The "gracings" temper this dimension/dynamic. In my book *Auguries,* I created the middle reality of the PROSPEROION to reflect/identify how we proper as a species with these two dimensions constantly a play. In brief, we find what holds us in place, centers us, makes for the existential embrace that gives us our alignment/belongsong candle glowing like a wand in the whirlwind.

The daily news – locally-worldly – is still do laced with predation of people on people, people on animals, people on the environment. Our diets are full of predatory killings. But so much predatory/prey activities of people against people. Such is the source of Evil in human existence. The source of the Good/God in our existence is from the prosperoion's centers that hold – like the breath in the wind, the person in the body—the trees through the seasons: the planet Earth with its revolutions around the sun. From the beginnings of humanity as a conscious species – the working with what holds-heals-embraces-sustains has allowed our evolution to now. The Hold became a consciousness that Holds. We've learned to use predation intelligently through animal domestication and agricultural needs. We have education-police-systems of justice and traditions of goodness to overcome the evil side of predatory actions. But the management of such is still an-every- culture-every-nation-every-town --- requirement to keep the centers holding. Music in all its forms are primal holding patterns. We hold our notes/sounds and structure them in patterns/forms where the center holds and we feel held in the hold. Alas, held/kept by harmonies. The magic of hugs is that we are held as we hug.

GOTMOL is about those gracing-hugs of our time that enhance-enable-enchant-enchoir the meaning of life in our time. Circumstances change, but the same ole challenge-response scenario prevails. I'm expecting any reader, if any, to have begun the process of tallying/rallying the gracings – yes the loves/beholds -- of their own life and to sense their own gracenote-belongsong as it plays in the symphony of life. Maybe this GOTMOL will enhance this sense of it all. I'm hoping so. It has been a TANG of TRUTH for me. THE HOLD is so real in everything. Perhaps what I've done here is but to grasp THE HOLD like old PROTEUS, who wouldn't prophesy until he could be held tight and true. Actually, I'm convinced beyond my ability to say so – that this is what we do to be as we are; and we've evolved to do it consciously unlike the oak tree, but of the same force. The spark of consciousness that seems to be in all species is that awareness of danger and predators. The ant on my counter-top scurries fast to get away from my finger. It also feels quite at home on that cookie.

In many words-terms-concepts, I have inserted the OiO or OIO to indicate that the dialogic reciprocity of life's contraries creates an illumination, and I, a prospering third dimension . . . candle in the wind that holds its fire. The symbol for this – The Syntangoion – I've explained rather thoroughly. In the make-up of existence it seems the interplay of "conscious/unconscious" – "observer/observed" -- "plus/minus" ---- and all the quantum interplays of wave/particle --- are illustrations of just how existence works to create matter and things (existences all) to hold-form and become what they are. It is the magical alchemy of existence that scientists are grasping to hold (like Proteus) so as to form a theory of everything: TOE to GUT to my poetries of the HEAD. Resilience By Design (REBDE) is a "gracing" phrase of all time, but with special challenges unique to our time. We can no longer use "God's Wrath" as an excuse/explanation for climate catastrophe, massive human mortality, the loss of species of fireflies and butterflies . . .due to our failing to worship such deity.

I should note here that the three main concepts of the universe all have THE HOLD in their constants and systems: the Standard Model with the Big Bang and endless expansion – the Fixed Model that all is as it is and will be – and the Cyclical Model that all will expand so far and then contract with the big crunch and begin again. (Perhaps "string theory" plays along with them all.)

Paul Davies in his THE LAST THREE MINUTES, Basic books, 1994 quotes Weinberg's conclusion in his First Three, namely – "that the more the universe seems comprehensible, the more it, also, seems pointless." Davies sees a "cosmic death" in the last three minutes. He concludes:

"If there is a purpose to the universe, and it achieves that purpose, then the universe must end, for its continued existence would be gratuitous and pointless. Conversely, if the universe endures forever, it is hard to imagine that there is any ultimate purpose to the universe at all. So cosmic death may be the price that has to be paid for cosmic success. Perhaps the most that we can hope for is that the purpose of the universe becomes known to our descendants before the last three minutes." (p.155)

More so today, it seems, the cyclical-bounce concept has generated some new looks. I'm in that camp a bit with my breathing – inhalation-hold-exhalation – scenario as a pervasive dynamic. Also, the concept of THE HOLD as a pervasive constant – has imaginatively contained within it the stretch-holding concept of the elastic band, which springs back rather than breaking. [Is this a "stretch" of string theory?] -- So much new data daily. The theorizing is well-fed. And, new more powerful telescopes and voyages are on the way. If we are careful and survival intelligent, we may have a better grasp way before those last three minutes. The GOTMOL is a *modus vivendi* that takes little theorizing to comprehend it. And, it doesn't need a purpose-concept of the universe to make it meaningful – even when it seems our manifest as a reflection of the manifest hold in existence for there to be any existence at all. Getting hold of ourselves is a very earthy-worthy thing – even if the universe couldn't care less. This Ah-Ha! "Something" seems an absolute grasping/surviving all polar annihilations.

Brian Greene concludes his ELEGANT UNIVERSE analysis of String Theory with this quote from Jacob Bronowski: ". . .in every age there is a turning point, a new way of seeing and asserting the coherence of the world." (p. 387) -- We are definitely at such a turning point. The search for that coherence and a way to express what we are finding goes on and on. My concept of THE HOLD does not appear in any book in my library. (Still searching.) And no where on the internet. It is a concept of "coherence" and what Fred Hoyle (The Nature of the Universe, 1950) referred to as "continuous creation," which would "play a role in the theories of the future."(p. 121, Mentor '55). – It's certainly integral to THE HOLD as I've expressed it in GOTMOL. Continuous creation is a "gracing" to every age and mind. Scientists, like poets/artists, are always climbing/composing ladders/energies of "structure."

ASSERTING THE WORLD'S COHERENCE

GRACING OUR TIME'S MEANING OF LIFE

How, therefore, to begin to tell this personal story as if a universal story? Unveil formulas elegant as any math. Yes, and to keep it simple and comprehensible. Indeed, as common as sunshine and rain, night-time and pain. Somehow, I must begin with the stirring surge of a Tsunami as it strives to become a major wave. Well, the major wave will have to be addressed as it gathers into itself and forces us to wake-up and, finally, its return to graceful lapping waves on the beaches of our time, personally, and TIME, existentially! Perhaps never so calm again!

Therefore, I perform as my own ICONIC entity in this *Theatrum Mundi*. I've no "fandom." (Like some.) I must audience and applaud myself -- as my own iconic "I" is under surveillance for its integrity, fire, and clarity of expression. – So, *Theatrum Mundi*'s wave rises: to a fullness and, then, the smoother flows on the beaches of our daily life, which is, now, more alert/aligned to the stirrings of a surge and the consequences. Saying "consequences" recalls the 2007 report The Age of Consequences, which examined climate and globalization issues—and the countries, politics, and sciences involved. Some are beginning to call current times The Beginnings of the Age of Catastrophe. Some leave out the word "beginnings" – to emphasize we are already there. There is, in fact, a Doomsday Calendar that gives us to about 2050 to stop the environmental-societal tsunami – or it will be out of our control. The glaciers are collapsing and melting as I write. The forest fires, the frequent mass floodings, the increase of damaging storms, and air and sea pollution are daily news items. Some Green New Deal seems the Real Heal Deal! The Tsunami, as death, destruction, catastrophe. shows itself every day. I'll get back to it, have to, but now to the "gracing" of life's meaning knowing it's there. Glaciers-Groceries-Gracings!!!

Glistenings from Songs of Dawn's Balm On The Lawn!

Therefore, the meaning of life will connect many current and probable issues at its core. My task is to connect what I see and live with – to some reciprocal sensing with existence in an unknowable universe and an increasingly vulnerable planet Earth and its life forms – including us. The always unknowable part is this: we don't know why there is existence or any clue to how it appeared --- if, indeed, it had to ever appear at all: it seems an eternal flux. Like stars and galaxies – we are in the dark. Astronomers and astrophysicists theorize daily. Telescopes give new data daily. There is as yet no TOE, theory of everything – or GUT, grand unified theory. I've added the HEAD – HOLISTOIONS EVOLUTIONARY ALIGNED DESTINY. (In Brief: *Hold Everything And Dance*.) I explore this HEAD concept in GOTMOL-- Gracing Our Time's Meaning of Life -- "our time's tango," because it is "ours" unlike any other. "Gracings" still form like dew to freshen life for its "behold" of "beauty." Gracings are as colorings, sun spangles ever-opening our eyes to see the wonderful promises of tomorrows. Therefore, the "holding becomings" of ourselves as gracenotes added to the symphony; adding our grace/place in the "accepting" music: our belongsong in the cacophony. Lucidities of – WE R!

Therefore, I begin the simple and comprehensible with the created word HOLISTOIONS. It's "holisto" is for wholism/holistic. The whole is larger than the parts. "Hold" is just that: the holding of the parts as a whole. You don't see it, but it's there! The stones create a structure that is more than the stones, but it is the "mortar" (both in mind and in sand): The Hold, holding the stones to Hold. The Craft and the Secret of the Freemasons can be summed in the bonding-holding-unifying concept of "mortar." Seems the use of a "mortar" goes as far back as 6500BCE. Such holdings make Fords and trees. Scientists don't yet have a TOE or GUT, but our meaning of life has to have a HEAD….that we Hold High: to grasp Beauty, Symmetry, Breakaways, Structures, and Thresholds. The craft-secret-&-magic-of-life is "things coming into themselves by belonging together." Once the "belong" of TO HAVE takes HOLD then the HEAD forms all existences – birds, trees, to humans. For any species to be the "fittest" – things have to align and "fit." For any species to reach its "epitome" (Epitofitme) all its HOLISTOIONS must align in their beheld/belong: a "holding's" sync/ synergistic/synaptic "grip" that nurtures progeny and survival.. O! Syncs of Epitofitme! Dancing Partners! TO HAVE AND TO HOLD! Asserting the Romance of Coherence! Hugging to the Music!

I'm not a scientist or occultist of any variety. I try to "ally-up" with scientific progress and theories, however. Nothing in my experience fits the category of occult. Daily, I am coached by life itself to speak really&poetically&spiritually of THE HOLD. It's amazing how two existences like hydrogen and oxygen can "grip" to form water. Once the right molecules get together – we have things like plastic, oak trees, dogs, and telescopes. So, there is something going on that causes processes to "tango" a holding pattern that HOLDS. Everything that exists(us) as an entity got that way because of that "something" that happens when things suddenly "belong together" and out pops a petunia and an onion. Seeds-Sperm-Ovaries!!! The desk I work at is composed of wood-iron-brass and more. My computer is a bunch of things working as a one thing. Call it magical, mysterious --- or any one of the theories of physicists – it is a fact that stuff and stars have their unique hold --- that we with our "consciousness" … "behold." A look at my zinnias or any book stirs one to say such are "Wonders To Behold." So, our consciousness does its own holding as thought – so to have all things in this world we have – take hold in the mind, as it were, so we can "handle" them. That oak tree, that tomato, that Toyota are Holding their own!

We humans are perhaps the only species(but watch a bird building its nest) whose hand/mind hold to put things together with a goal in mind for the sync of the parts and utility. Coronavirus is testing that capability now. Scientists all over the globe are trying to find what holds to defeat this contagion pandemic. We have what it takes – but we have to find what takes hold to perform as needed. Once we have hold of it – it will hold. – Alas, as I'm writing this (8/14/20), I read on my iPhone this headline from the University of Chicago: "Quantum States Can Now Be Held 10,000 Longer Than Before." And so it is that this new capability will advance quantum research in many ways. [One thought, for some tomorrow, is that as we as a species became able (under water first) to hold/control our breath: this holding focused - "consciousness" became our "Threshold." Once controlling "thought"-- our sense of "self" manifested through holdings of breath&thought. Breath held oxygenates our blood. Thus, there snapped-in-to-place the synapses in our brains.]

---- Now, some holding-essentials for the GOTMOL of our world at today's turning point, before the Tsunami gathers uncontrollably. The manifest GOTMOL through all, is simply to protect/ comprehend/hold-onto (PROCOHOTO) GRACING OUR TIME'S MEANING OF LIFE. O! The GOTMOL PROCOHOTO of the EPITOFITME of it all. I don't seek to over-work these amalgamized neologisms. They serve the purpose if they heighten-brighten the need to see/feel that our time is different and that new comprehensions/expressions are inevitable: to find what belongsongs HOLD us up and ready to go -- Now! Such seek the ANSWER – A New Spirituality We R! So, dear reader, feel free to go do your own neologistic amalgamations. Become your own self-Illumination and Icon of I am that I am. So, this dotting of one's own "i" means I must begin the "gracings" with a review of the origin and meaning of the SYNTANGOION. But first Apollo then 'APO'KSTROPHES'.

APOLLO, with his lyre, is a good place to begin to see the power of three at work since three is the primal-archetype of THE HOLD. The lyre in this rendering was no doubt an original three string lyre: each string named as Nete-Mesh-Hypate. These personifications came from the first three Muses – Aoide-Melete-Mneme. These three were soon tripled into the Nine Muses. Zeus had children in three sets – Fates-Graces-Muses: the Graces were three – Beauty-Grace-Charity. Not far from the Greeks were the Etruscans in Italy and they had three main deities – Tinia-Uni-Menrva which became Jupiter-Juno-Minerva in the Roman Empire: and later – God-Jesus-Holy Spirit and three crosses on the hill. Meanwhile over in India there were the Hindu three – Brahma-Siva-Vishnu at the center. The story goes on and on -- seconds-minutes-hours, subject-object-predicate, sing-sang-sung, mother-father-child, past-present-future, etc. etc. etc. Some say the numbers 3—6---9 carry the secret of existence, since they are three numbers, each divisible by 3 – 1,2,3 times and multiples of 3. When you add the three together you get 18, which is divisible by all three. In the Jewish tradition the number 18 is meaningful/lucky: CHET (8) & YED (10) = 18 CHAI – which is LIFE. – And, since my writer's domain is called AFIRADAPO (A FIREFLIES AT DAWN POIESIS), I should note the three genera of Fireflies: Photinus-Photuris-Pyractomena – in the Domain of Eukaryota. And, yes, matter is three: solid-liquid-gas. Don't forget the three performances of the Greek Chorus – Strophe-Antistrophe-Epode. Somehow this led to an Ode called an Apostrophe. All this and so much more put the three apostrophes in 'Apo'kstrophes'! – Hey! Galaxies are three: spiral-elliptical-irregular. And the primal soup was three: protons-neutrons-electrons. Thus, on-and-on to all the "hold-ons." – The word "strophe" means a "turning." I say a turning to address-being addressed-at this address. ADDRESSOR/ADDRESSEE/ADDRESSOION. *The Trinity I grew-up with is on the back cover: One Nation Undivided, With Liberty And Justice For All. That Triple Address guided me Upon The Earth- not Under someone's God.* – At India's Prayagrai, the Hindus gather at the three holy rivers: Ganges-Yamuna & the "mystical" SARASWATI – flowing like a "poet's" apostrophe, the Syntangoion's lantern-glow of IAM : Liberty's lifted torch of Freedom.

4

'APO'KSTROPHES'

Now, you've a grasp, you with your three names, how the three apostrophes appear in 'Apo'kstrophes'. The poetic structure/address called an "Apostrophe" is embedded therein, because, it is the address to that which addresses. Both of which happen at this HOME Address – Humanity's Own Mother Earth. So there is this triune address function. So, with these underpinnings, I will take this GOTMOL to now consider 'Apo'kstrophes'. Of course, this rings the bells of Euripides to the Pleiades and Socrates to Galaxies. And the three apostrophes sing like the Greek choruses of glories and catastrophes revealed from the nature of existence and signed in these three address signatures of the human drama. It's an interesting note that the binary-digital world can't handle the apostrophe – mauling it's simplicity -- it's-can't-won't -- into forms as this: "don’t" – sometimes as 47 and 48. My favorite: MDO'KELLY. So 'Apo'kstrophe's could email as -- ’Apo'kstrophes“. My name seems to have got its apostrophe when the British, overtaking the Celtic world in 14th Century, with its sounds and signatures, heard a strange hold in the way they pronounced their names. Then, there was that comma-like mark above the Gaelic O. Just move it down like this O'K. Thus, one origin of the apostrophe in names and language. Seems it progressed as follows: Ua – O – O'. There were others such as the Italian edition of Petrarch in 1509 and a French printer G. Tory in 1529. By the 17th Century the O's and Mac's were dropped so names would be more English. Many kept the O as my immigrant ancestors and Nationalists into 20th Century.

So, why this bit of history if but to emphasize that an apostrophe has three uses: *possessive* nouns, *omissions* of letters, *plurals* of letters, numbers, and symbols. (And it belies technology.) Which, strangely, recalls the physicists and their magic-three-digit-ratio of 1/137: the gist of which I'm not able to grasp (but then they have problems, too). However, the number seems to significantly relate three major domains of physics: electromagnetism in the form of the charge of an electron, relativity in the form of the speed of light, and quantum mechanics in the form of Plank's constant. In all of this, protons and electrons are bound by interactions with photons. (See Feynman's "The Mysterious 137." Another trinity in our 3-D world. Three primes each only divisible by one and itself; together they add to 11 which divides the same. 3 is the ultimate prime. The magic of The Hold in primes.) The Old Testament had three: Torah-Nebiim-Ketubim. 3 Crosses on the hill! Seems, since the 4th Century BCE that triple spirals and trinity knots-- Triquetra-Triskelion-Walknut-Trefoil knot, etc. have functioned as the oldest symbol of spirituality: mind-body-soul.

TIMELY NOTES ON THE HOLDING THOUGHTS OF THE HOLD

A week after writing the above about the magical ratio of 1/137, I found a 12/4/20 article in Popular Mechanics, which featured a Quanta Magazine article entitled – "Physicists Nail Down the 'Magic Number' That Shapes the Universe." I'll briefly summarize and quote here and there.

The number is called Alpha and is the Fundamental-Fine-Structure-of-the Universe…such that if it were any smaller or any bigger --- we-earth-existence might not be here and probably not. The number: 1/137.035999206 – with an uncertainty factor of 0.000000011. [I note the numbers in both, past the decimal point, are 9: the main ratio of the 3 numbers add-up as 11. Alas, 9-3-11 are ever so in the primal sequence of 3-5-7-9-11.

"The fine-structure constant was introduced in 1916 to quantify the tiny gap between two lines in the spectrum of colors emitted by certain atoms. . . .The fine structure constant . . . has no dimensions or units." (Such as meters per second or miles per hour as measuring the speed of light.) "It's a pure number that shapes the universe to an astonishing degree. A 'magic number" that comes to us with no understanding. . . .The constant is everywhere because it characterizes the strength of the electromagnetic force affecting charged particles such as electrons and protons." There are three ways of determining the fine-tuned hold of this constant: "ultra-precise measurements" -- the basis of this article -along with particle colliders and telescopes to determine the fundamental structure-dynamics of the universe. [Three Ways!]

This is on-going work for the GUT-TOE & HEAD of it all. Being no physicist or mathematician, I but see the holistoion THE HOLD at work that combines, unites, and coheres existences to be what they are and to be the "somethings" that hold their held to belong in space-time until the hold is released by whatever random or internal/external parameters of causation. Much of an answer seems to lie in the realm of DARK MATTER, which is non-luminous-invisible-particle realm, but seems to be the "glue" holding galaxies together and that "gravitationally sculpt the cosmos as a whole." Theories abound!

I've called it THE HOLD which is, indeed, a magical thing – ephemeral-existential/ transcendent-immanent. We know it's there in everything – because nothing would be if "nothing" held it together. Alas! SOMETHING's holding-on. The fact that we can hold, behold, and be held – is perhaps the greatest "gracing" of our meaning of life. It is most certainly a direct connect to the magical glue of nature: stars to species to soups. This book, GOTMOL, bounces around in this arena of ALPHA as an 'Apo'kstrophes' gathering the gracings, singin gracenotes into the symphony -- with all the groceries of our greenest blessings. Hopefully, you'll saddle-up this steed and keep the reins in your hands as I unfold/enfold this "magic" the physicists are trying to grasp. Prophesy: the future of human meaning – planetary/biological/cosmic -- will find it greatest "foothold" as this "magic" is unfurled and composed. It will be the star player (finest constant) in the our-time wrestles of Consequences-Compassion-Consciousnesses. This ALPHA IDENITY – as Fundamental Life Structure -- will seek equilibrium with AI and our machine-to-machine future.

Ahh! Things to hold in mind as GOTMOL unfolds some grasps of what holds.

AH-HA! The SYNTANGOION of 'APO'KSTROPHES'!

Recall, that these three *alpha* apostrophes and signature of 'Apo'kstrophes' are formed from the Greek terms "apokatastasis"(restoration); "apokaluptein" (reveal/disclose-apocalypse); "apokryphos" (hidden/secret-apocrypha). (See ALTARPIECES for this. Is this the origin of A-OK & OKAY!?) I've re-touched these many bases, because this 'Apo'kstrophes' refers to the dimensions of the "onomatopoetic" – ever seeking the truer sound, the soundest thought -- "metacosmesis" – the renewal of the world in one's own time and "aletheia" that uncovers reality's truths. Ah-Ha! The primal sounding "Ahh" of AUM and birth just out of the womb!! Thus, an earthly POIETIS in concert with a cosmic POIESIS to create the POIEMA of our "earthly" voice and crafted poetries. That ever-thresholding-passage to grasp what Holds to be Held.

THE POIOEMA! POIOESIS!

I am an 'Apo'kstrophes' of the Poioema's Poioesis – and have so signatured that human endeavor to strum the strings of reality to hold for their truest, most harmonious/resonant music and thought. I'm not alone. All this is relevant to Gracing Our Time's Meaning of Life. OK is the Odyssean Kairos of the GOTMOL – that ever-now journey to capture the fruits of our Earth at their best. And, now, Apocalypse on horizon! Look out! The Tsunami is rising.

[Pause a moment to note this. Below, I include a mini-essay on songs that deal with WIND to give a poetic feel for what's "Blowing in the Wind." Here, I mention two songs that represent the Tsunami-Apocalypse challenge of today – the positive side and the negative side of our present mind-set. The first is Elton John's NEVER TOO LATE from the 2019 movie Lion King. The second is Andrew Lloyd Webber's FAR TOO LATE from his new production of Cinderella due for Broadway in 2021. I was not "overly impressed" with their renditions I listened to on the internet. – But they do reflect the two sides of today's tsunami of climate-cultural change crises. On the one hand – it's never too late to take our stand and do it right. On the other, we are faced with the scientists who say it's getting "far too late" to change the fall of the dominoes. Webber has even commented that this was on his mind. His song concludes:

If I run to You – If I begged you to forgive me – We might share a different fate
But it is far too late- Far too late to sing a love song –
You're in someone else's arms.

We are in the arms of Climate Earth. The Solar Wind's in our hair. Must sing our love song as never before in the arms of technology/AI. Nicholas Carr in his "Glass Cage" says we had better be careful or AI will take over. Once AI's controllers control – we are in their arms: freedom gone. We will have lost control of The Hold. Tsunami at the Turning Point! GOTMOL de-graced!? It's not-too-late! Sunsets awake to shake The Dawn's Balm on the Lawn.

The following Dialogue between Prophet and the Soul to be read as dialogue between Earth and Humanity. . .and variations on that theme.

FROM PROPHET & SOUL DIALOGUE (2014) IN SYMPATHIES, P. 140,144:

PROPHET --I'm just you're every-day prophet:
trainer in your corner, keys in your pocket.
No *ludere cum sacris,* just serious *buddhi*!
Hands-on, *dichetal do chennaid's* my duty;
that spontaneity St. Patrick said was OK,
and *teinm laegda* to find the said, finesse the say.
I'm Amos, Cathbad, Jefferson and Confucius:
a cereal bowl of Gnosis to awaken your Venus.
I'm your lunch-pail Shekinah and Innerer Klang"
l'enchanteur and le echanteur, both hands:
natura naturata and natura naturans.
I underpaint your canvass to glow the stimmung;
give your *summa summarum* its sing, sang, sung.
I've no magical verses mystical or mythical.
I've no poetical verses eternal or scriptural.
But I rhyme enough with profit,
the axis in Abraxas,
to keep a Soul on top of it.
    "You Are The Song,
    I am The Word. Sing it!"
SOUL -- OK! I get the message. My answer's forming.
Illumination glows with the fireflies
hands caress what would fizzle-out in jars:
that glow from the seas, the sun, the stars.
I must open-up the attic, air-out the basement.
spring-clean the house and refresh the pond.
. . . . A care felt in that clutch of mane and sweat,
that sureness of hooves clawing earth and sea.
I must believe in the ride, that I'll make it home,
learn the song, the words, the music. Sing it!
My Phoenix and Tundra Swan are in Dag's Chariot
pulled aloft by the "Shining Mane."
I'm re-feeling my own faith in myself;
to trust without saddle, reins, or trusted spurs.
My arms fluttering like wings in the jumps
on a stallion's grace against the tides.. . . . . . .
    "I write the songs – That make the Whole World Sing.
    I write the Songs of Love and Special Things."

Domenico Fetti's – A Classical Poet
An 'Apo'kstrophes' As Any Homer-Virgil

Each age sounds a call to cadence balance;
Line rhythmic meaning with which souls can bind.
We barely compose our brilliance to cope,
If memory's voice fades from crafted hope.

As our parade rhymes its burn with the dawn,
To timings that sing again and again ----
Like flicks into flares off some eternal flint stone's
Tone of tunings round poetry's fire.

I love your feel –
Visitations syntaxed with spine shivers
And thoughts wooed to life like shoots in the night,
Memories arrowed to the heart of day:
Guest with me on a magic carpet ride.

[My Quatrains from "A Craft to Haunt" --"What's A Poem" --"Guest With Me"]

HOMER   **VIRGIL**

THE SYNTANGOION

I've explained this symbol in various texts before. But now I'm giving its sway in the Meaning of Life. Bear with me as I repeat myself a bit. And, as I do, hopefully reaching some new harmonies, please know that its meaning holds the magic of life's meaning as I've experienced it. At the heart of existence is the interaction, interpenetration, reciprocillation of opposites –– represented by two circles engaging to release a tertiary (tertium quid) dimension of illumined-inspired individualism: that third thing formed into all the entities of existence. It is obvious, since existence and we exist, that these two realms – say matter/anti-matter – don't annihilate to nothing. The attraction is unavoidable: plus and minus attract, but don't become some static freeze. Something breaks that seize of symmetry. Scientists are now calling that "something" – AXIONS. Such are "imagined" energies that hold onto matter so that it survives and makes way for hydrogen and oxygen to form water. So that big I Candle-Flame created by the interaction is the flaring-up of mattered existences – gives a "let there be light" to everything that is. Alas, the shining countenances of YOU-ME-US – in a "generation" I've aptly named GEN-i-US. Therefore, in this context let's say AXOIONS!

Here's the other allied comprehension of this engagement – Something&Nothing. The core dynamic: everything entails/embodies/yin-yang opposites. The concept of nothing entails its opposite of something and vice versa. There is no plus without a minus and vice versa. No male without female. No life without death. No night without day. ETC. In brief, so long as there is the active domain of AXOIONS or PROTOPHOBIC BOSONS – existence will always exist – but as life erupts so is death built-in to it. Flames can be blown-out. Sparks on the fly can ignite another illumination in the dark. HOLD-ON! You, the emergent IAM THAT IAM! The TANG twixt Yin&Yang. The Singing twist the Song & the Sung. How sweet it is!

Entanglement is not so "spooky." It's easily comprehended. Each of the circles embodies each other (interacting or not), because there is no conceiving one (ahh the womb of it) without the other. Indeed, everything would be in a static-freeze-ever-annhilating condition if not for some Big Bang-Tremulous Tang grabbing hold of itself in the annhilations. Ahh twixt Anima and Animus arises Animate. LIFE! HOLOHOLDS! – In my Trilogy, I described how the interplays of

Predation-Procreation – give rise to the Prosperoion: which is life that existentially prospers and consciously strives to hold on to what prospers. Thus, the dotted "i" candle burning its "tang" in the dark. "And there was light!" Life's I AM from polar confrontations.

Now, if that HOLISTOIONS doesn't take you back to the Council of Nicea, 325 CE, then I'll just repeat myself again. (See AUUGURIES, p.207) Theologians sought to play the word HOMOOUSIOS of Athanasius, where the two adjacent Os meant Father&Son are as one and the same. Arius preferred HOMOIOUSIOUS. He stuck that "Iota" in there to indicate they were "similar"-- not "like." So this may have been the first stirrings in me of OIO becoming the SYNTANGOION. Even so, there was so much before, as referenced above, in dualist/tertiary thought and so much after in the theories of today's physicists. This symbol is inclusive of all these graphics on the nature of existence. So, when I write POP[A]POP/MOM[A]MOM – that [A} is as much Arius as Arion-Aristophanes-Aristotle-Axion-Aoide – as the current 'Apo'kstrophes'. Those three apostrophes include this trinity of OIO. Call me MOIOKE! Call the winds MOIORA!

[To add to the recipe, here's some "oio" dimensions from Heidegger's "Metaphysics." He discusses the Greek word "homoiois" as the assimilation/accommodation of things coming out of hiding, as it were, and attaining perceivable correctness of being. Then, there's this other term "zoion" – which means animal – and more cogently as in this formula: *anthropos = zoion logon echon* – which means "man, the animal equipped with reason." I prefer the term "creature," but this adds some spice and also gives the origin of the word "Zoo." And, I like that "OIO" as "things coming out of hiding" to "correctness of being." Also, note Heidegger's, and others, concept of BE – ING entails a HOLD – INGS in order for something TO BE what it is. OIO is often pronounced as "oie" in a term.]

The three sectioned SYN-TANGO-ION, breaks down to Syn-tang-go-i-on as a five-sound word. Each sound has a meaning. "Syn"(sync-synergy-synaesthesia) the "tang" as that epiphanic burst of Ah-Ha! "Tango" is the rhythmic dance of life – "i" is that me/you----"on" is of the suffix "ion" that means alive and acting now. (This symbol, on Frontispiece of GOTMOL, shows three vibrations on either side of "I" – the arch's Keystone -- a manifestation of the number 7 as Threshold-Gateway: see my 7 Villanelles in POP. Chakras, anyone!? The prime 5 has much the same (toe-hold) play in THE HOLD.)

Ah, five! Another primal number as in five fingers, five toes, five weekdays and a sense of that something called a quintessence. Ah! Theorists are once again forming a fifth force of nature. AH-HA!!! All is so connected to the "quintessential" QUINTETOION breathing sequence – with its five instruments and seven sounds. (See pyramids, below.) But first to address this fifth force of nature – the FIFORONAT. [Keeping in mind the five primal numbers -- 3-5-[7]-9-11 – each an odd number, with a single mid mark (as a keystone – like the 7 in this group) and equal marks down each side. Oddions are important in that they represent breaks of symmetry, as equal numbers are, and form a foundation—an arch a threshold a gateway. These will show-up again later. All of this is "first" discussed on my website. In this primal group of seven where each is divisible by 1 and itself…except for 9, which is also divisible by 3, thus three numbers: just another numbers game of 3 and 9. I'm hoping to live to 93 and plan for 99.]

This symbol, recently discovered, is the closest "ancient" suchness I've seen to my Syntangoion. It utilizes the Greek letter "phi" which is basically an I in the middle of an O. (The PHI symbol conveys ideas of consciousness, philosophy, and Golden Ratio. Seems to have come from the time of the dialogues concerning Democracy as found in Plato and Aristotle. Aristotle gives the concepts of POLITERA (the people)—POLIS (the State) and POLITY (the common ground of equal distribution.) Similar to my Syntangoion discussion – the reciprocillation of dialogue creates a centering holding pattern. Plato's Republic and Aristotle's Politera were the Political life concepts of Athens. There seems to be no information on who created this symbol or when. But the literature reviewed thus far makes it a symbol of Dialogic Democracy. The Unitarian Universalist symbol of the two circles (the one and the many) with Liberty's flaming chalice/torch of knowledge and personal creativity/consciousness -- has, no doubt, been an influence. The concept is integral to the "holding-illuminating-forming" processing of human consciousness—and existence being as it is. My Syntangoion takes a few dance steps and our daily holding pattern existence a bit beyond within the POANSWER – Poetries Of A New Spirituality We R. That "R" --beyond Religion's past -- to be the renewed 3R's of Renaissance-Resilience-Reverence of humanity and planet. All Hail! – the new songs while dawn's on the lawn. And, see! That candle's HELD in THE HOLD.

Before I got into the current FIFORONATS, I was comprehending the fifth instrument in the QUINTETOION – first calling it "silence." But later realizing that -- while there was that silence – often not always – from one sequence to the next-- it was really a HOLD: the breath was HELD. Just like a note of music. Just take a deep breath and HOLD it before releasing. This is in full on my website. "AH---HA"---"CHI"----"A---U---M"---"JAAHHH!" These seven sounds from four instruments --- the fifth being THE HOLD connected to each. I used the symbol of the pyramid – with its four sides HELD by the fifth, as base, on the ground. [When I meditate/Quintetoion, I put each thumb between its four fingers. The Hold! Arch! Grip! Threshold! This seeming aside is relevant here, because THE HOLD (howsoever it happens) seems the fifth force of nature, because it holds all the other forces in unison to enact things that hold together: cardinals, carrots, galaxies. If we could not hold our breath then we would not have control over it. Nature/the Universe needs that FIFORONAT so to hold processes long enough so something HOLDS (fits) and an existence is formed. Always, the issue before the scientists – is – how did matter form and hold on rather than the absolute annihilation of opposites leaving nothing? Then comes the theory of "matter photons," which act as "messengers" beyond oblivion. Then comes the concept of AXOIONS which allow for a hold of matter – such that matter thus HELD becomes existence of stars and us. It's a constant labor of physicists to correctly theorize how matter survived to be us....to Hold!!

So, the theory that has my current attention – is that existence seems structured as a breathing sequence of in and out -- with a holding that forms and keeps matter together: promoting life that breathes. All life had this triune sequence of in—hold—out. I put the four forces of nature, two as "in" and two as "out" – with the fifth as both between and holistically embracing. --- So, briefly, the FIFORONAT is that "quintessence" (called the "Pentameroion" in AUGURIES) that holds on to matter so existence as we know it has a gateway to exist. And that "as we know it" is due to a controlled consciousness that can HOLD its thought and know it. This is the daily experience of COVNAT our covenantal hold/hug/caress with others/nature. And, yes, there seems to be a "holding pattern" sameness between our COVNAT and the FIFORONAT. Becomings find belonging . . . and hold! Physicists working in these dimensions are now in the grasp of how "consciousness" plays a role in our grasp of the quantum world: where we as measuring observers hold to a perception being a wave or a particle. Seems THE HOLD is so physically-psychically connected in the quantum world as in our daily 3-D world. Much-much more to come about this connection. [One thinks "atmosphere" "heliosphere" "magnetosphere" holding Earth. Add to these the concept of the INTERSTITIUM, which is now theorized as an "organ" of the body – in that (like our external skin) it holds around all internal organs in a nourishing-protective kind-of-way. Still learning! Just read an article by Paul Ratner (9/27/20—BIG THINK) about Vitaly Vanchurin's possible TOE candidate that the universe, physical laws of all reality around us, functions like a computer neural network. These neural networks mimic the way biological neural networks process and pass information signals that connect as networks that make things be as they are. Synapses everywhere. Yes! That's a Zebra. That's a proton. Still learning!].

Ah! To possess neural networks that know thought and breathing as a connected network – is to become conscious of one's self as a candle holding in the wind. Out of THE HOLD comes a HOLDING PATTERN that knows itself. Creatures from Ants to Zebras have a creature awareness, but no self-conscious-grasp of the HOLD as such and the language opportunity it presents. Ahhh! The feeling of being embraced. [Though the family dog does pretty well. And homing pigeons know the HOLD of where to go! We could hardly sing if we couldn't hold a note and sound a meaning!] So: knowing/experiencing THE HOLD -- humanity can build/conceive what holds – from a fire to family to a song -- to today's manufacturing of everything we have and to the technology of computers ever-ascending. We've come a long way from that first fire to 5G; the planet a rock to a rock that holds water and living forms abundantly: a COVENANTOION. ["Soul" is that inner/outer sense of holding&being held as a "me." Spirituality: conscious "souling" as "we are." "Interstitium!" O! Epitofitme! O! Embrace! O! Song of Sing Sang Sung! Beholds of the Hold's belongings together harmoniously. We can see the murmurations of starlings, but don't know how they hold it all together so.] Such Holds are full of magic. Any day is so!

The sciences can foresee earth's and our final days if we don't "grasp" our planetary challenge. All hands are committed to this "spirit" as saviors of human existence. We (generation of GEN-i-US) on the crest of the rising wave, can augur the future. We can smooth/control the rising Tusunami by education/commitment beyond STEM to include the three R's of Renassiance-Resonance-Reverence. WEWEWE singing RERERE all the way home. Yes! — Renascence's Rational Reverence for Life: rebirth-renewal-resolve -- that synchronous-holding vibration of victorious vitality. – Now, on the Look-Out! It's a slipping precipice – watching feet-slip and stones plunge into the abyss. Apocalypse on the horizon! Contagions filling the hospitals and bodybags!!

PAUSE. REFLECT. WHAT'S HAPPENED OF NOTE SO FAR?

We, astride the ever-galloping-poetic Arion/Arion (immortal poet/immortal horse) - now merged as AROION) -- prancing-dancing-singing through the SHOALS of WONTSUNODI in our COVNAT – those Shining Holds of Angelic Legacies of Wonders That Should Not Die --- in our Covenant with Nature: and this symbolized as the synched-caress-dance of SYNTANGOION – and its hold told-bold by the helds of 'Apo'kstrophes'! -- Alas, a MOIOKE astride an AROION breathing fully the QUINTETOION while pondering the AXOIONS of the FIFORONAT from an iPhone story along with the progress of the coronavirus throughout the species of planet earth this very moment of 9/9/20. --- From ancient times to today, humanity is still grasping for the meaning of life in the midst of inevitable/daily death. DeathInLife[A]LifeInDeath or LifeInDeath[A]DIL is an ever-spinning-swinging palindrome pendulum of the beating pulse. Mystic dreamings of the past become the computerized telescopes of today. So we really know today that all we are and have been and are to become, happens on a speck of dust in an incomprehensible vastness of darkness and ceaseless collisions of things in the night of unimaginable space and beingness with no seeming goal but to blast away until there is nothing but nothing. Such seems to be the case - so far. – Those polarizations are in constant DILALID[A]DILALID reciprocity -- with 'Apo'kstrophes' in the middle. The tsunami of planetary death is ever rising its ever-presence. Resilience Here vs. Rebirth There is moving spiritualty forward. Hold-On for a steady gallop! – The US, as Universal Spirituality, is an Our Time "gracing" by our GEN-i-US.

I left the corporate world in 1962 and tested to enter the University of Chicago, to study philosophy, history of religions, and liberal/humanistic Unitarian ministry. I decided for ministry. I saw myself as a champion for freedom, reason, the meaning of life and as a poetic-celebrant of life's most glorious achievements and our most cherished moments. This, with the best of beauty-goodness-truth for standing tall before the inevitabilities of death and pain. Thus, creating a well-held life of significant meaning and worth--- most of the time. Now, since I have "more" time, I'm writing my best "say" of the meanings found in my wrestle with the meaning of life. None follow me as some version of Illuminati as I move onward and I don't expect the remotest smidgen of a fandom as I stride forward. What I write is for me to have said so and writ so with the pride of integrity and as much artistry as I could muster. I'm paying for it, too! I have no "critics" or positive "reviewers." A precious few have read "some." I'll write till done! "No Time To Die"-- title of next 007 movie due in 2021. (My double OO is sometimes a 7 as on Frontispiece of this book.) Title suits me. Favorite love song: "Till The End of Time." [Sung now as "Full Moon & Empty Arms."] Brian Greene just published "Until The End Of Time." "Time on my hands!" Time's a human measure! The universe couldn't care less. So, these terms to define/declare/decode the SYNTANGOION.

HOLISTOION -- AXOION – MOIOKE- AROION – QUINTETOION – COVENATOION – POIOEMA !!! (Pronounced – PO – EYE – O – ee – MAH). None may ever make it to a dictionary. That's not the point. Stuff I write may never be read to a consequence. Oh, yes – and the KOSMOSOION MYSTEXSOION and our PROSPEROION. Don't forget HUMANOION and ARIELOION. Alas, one of my favorite terms is best said as a palindromion: AWEAEWA--Augural Wisdom Energies/ EWA. (Pronounced: Ahh—Wee – Ahh–Eee–Wahh! AWEAEWA MOMZIEKAI POIOEMAS!!!Recall the PENTAMAROION of AUGURIES: same family as the FIFORONAT.

– In all, the polarities are in ever-spinning reciprocillations to form identities which stand, hold, and flame on their own: Adam/Eve, apples, trees, snakes, etc. That "I"—incantation-intuition-illumination-identity-intimations of -I AM. In what follows, the term ANEMOION (planetary winds at one's back/to winds in the face – a-nee-mo-e-on) will be added.

Recall how OiO relates to the quantum polarity of Observer and Observed to create "holding patterns" of "information." This interaction is unavoidable when "grasping" (hand and mind) the realities of existence. IT and WE form an US. See! There's that blazing I AM Candle in the center of it all! I think Homer-Plato-Aristotle-Virgil-Voltaire—along with the UU Flaming Chalice world would approve. So, too, the Hanukkah mid candle SHAMASH, which lights the Menorah's other eight, like a pendulum left to right/right to left till all nine are lit. Alas, all these sources would join the following choir of songs.]

Having discusses the FIFORONAT the QUINTETOION the INTERSTITIUM the PENTAMAROION all with a dimension of QUINTESSENCE – I offer this way of conceiving all of this in the context of THE HOLD. Here is this format of existence: [(+/-) (-/+) (+/+) (-/-)]These four gathered polarities in their superpositions and obvious "spookinesses" – are encased by the brackets of THE HOLD as the fifth dimension. Poetically, I guess, this is a picture of the Quintessential Quintessence of THE HOLD.

THE AMAZING GRACE OF CANDLES IN THE WIND

In revising the context of A New Spirituality We Are, time to discuss two songs and their revisions. This is done to embody grace in the brevity of human life. The Newton/Rees classical Christian hymn "Amazing Grace" had all the theologies of "the Lord's promise," "God's praise," and a sense of "shall possess" a life beyond the veil. This contrasts to the much more modern version as sung by Judy Collins, which eliminated those theologies, but retained the concept of "Grace," which has "brought us"("me" Newton) safe thus far – And Grace will lead us home." Here's the third verse of both, Collins' word in ():

> Through many dangers, toil, and snares
> I(We) have already come:
> 'Twas grace hath brought me(us) safe thus far,
> And grace will lead me (us) home.

Clearly a move from individual salvation to that of humanity – and that survival carrying within that something called "grace" as potential and protocol of promise fulfilled. Indeed, a song that's sung: a homing finding home. An amazing grace, indeed, if its feel/find of glory can be transferred from transcendence to immanence: from theology to global humanity. So, when I write of "gracings" and "Graceoions" – I'm tuned by a humanistic resonance that Humanity is now charged with to comprehend on a global scale – for Earthly-salvation-survival, [A 'Grace' definition: things coming into themselves by belonging together. Religions don't own grace, which is a human experience long before institutions.] "Candle in the Wind" is an Elton John composition/performance. It first appeared as a 'goodbye' song to so-early-dead Marilyn Monroe. Years later, 1997, he revised it for the so-early-dead Princess Diana. Here's the mid-lyric with the Diana change in ():

> And it seems to me you lived your life
> Like a candle in the wind
> Never knowing who to cling to
> (Never fading with the sunset)
> When the rain set in
> And I would have like to have known you
> (And your footsteps will always fall here)
> But I was just a kid
> (Along England's greenest hills)
> Your candle burned out long before
> Your legend ever did.
> (Your legend ever will.)

It seems so often to me that our lives are like candles in the wind – as we fight for our flourish of flame knowing the wind soon will win – and blow us out. Yet there is a "grace" in the living challenge of it all: that "belonging" something that feels like home, with its warming, glowing, and crackling hearth fire consummation of wonders to behold.—These recall the Parsons/Rogers duet "Islands in the Stream" in MOM's poem "O! Why Write a Love Poem Now?" The flowing theme of the Muse of Mortality was this COVID-19 time. O! The Amazing Grace of Candles in the Wind: Holding-Holding like Islands in the Stream. O! A time for re-visioning is upon us. O! Syntangoion!

SO WHAT IS THIS……………..BUT…………

THE EARTHARIAN EPIC MASTERSONG OF ICONIC HEROS AND

ONTOLOGICALLY AUTHENTIC MANIFESTS OF A NEW CONSCIOUSNESS.

I wish! Well, perhaps, a real tune/grasp, howsoever small, of some Holding Pattern frequencies within such a Mastersong's reverbs of reason-resilience-reverence. A sounding of gracenotes into the gracing GRACE of beauty and promises fulfilled in the human composition and performance on life's ever-ready-ever-expanding stage of interacting realities manifesting a belongingness that holds to be it's own cohesive-formed—knitted-caressed-held reality.

Now, I must take a swerve. California-Oregon-Washington-Colorado-Australia & Africa's Amazon forests – are on fire. This reality, with COVID-19, is happening right now. The song, "Candle in the Wind," suddenly has more play. The Santa Ana, Santa Lucia, and Diablo winds are fueling a mega swath of wildfires (called climate fires now) that are consuming, towns, home, villages, lives, and millions of forest acres. And the Derechos of the mid-West. Hurricanes and tornadoes from the Gulf. So, "Wind" songs have come to mind.

Prior to "Candle in the Wind"(1973), was the song "They Call the Wind Maria"- from the Broadway Musical "Paint Your Wagon"(1951) and then the film in 1969 with Harve Presnell singing it. These lyrics began the song:

> A way out here they got a name for rain and wind and fire…
> The rain is Tess the fire Joe and *they call the wind Maria. . .*
> Maria blows the stars around and sends the clouds a flyin. . .
> Maria makes the mountains sounds like folks were up there dying.
> (*Maria! Maria! They call the Wind Maria!*.......Blow my love to me.)
> *[I sang the whole song -10/5/2020 - for my family at Marilyn's birthday celebration.]*

Those mountains-forests are aflame apocalyptically today with the winds whipping infernos everywhere with sounds of homes and people dying-crying. In 1988 Bette Midler sang the "Wind Beneath My Wings," -- and sang it to the world at the 9/11 Memorial in 2001. (I'm writing this on 9/11/20.) This is the main chorus in this song composed in 1982 by Silbar and Henley:

> Did you ever know that you're my hero
> And everything I would like to be?
> I can fly higher than an eagle
> For you are the wind beneath my wings….
> You, you, you, you are the wind beneath my wings.

Now, to these three – Candle in the Wind – They Call the Wind Maria – and The Wind Beneath My Wings," I add a fourth – Bob Dylan's "Blowing in the Wind" of 1962 – with these lyrics:

> Yes, 'n' how many years can a mountain exist
> Before it is washed to the sea?
> Yes, 'n' how many years can some people exist
> Before they're allowed to be free?
> Yes, 'n' how many times can a man turn his head
> And pretend that he just doesn't see?
> The answer, my friend, is blowin' in the wind.
> The answer is blowing in the wind.

There's a major "address" spewing from each of these songs. "Blowing in the Wind" rather sums it all: the planet the peoples the promises of tomorrow are under siege as the climate changes throw hurricanes, storms and mass evacuations due to wind-whipped uncontrollable fires. And, all this, now – as the Covid-19 contagion increases its pandemic dimensions. It's a terrible time on planet earth! The winds of it all become all the more disastrous if we humans don't hear the winds, the howlings of freedom, listen to the scientists, and change our lifestyles as a species. Alas, feel/know the wind beneath our wings!

I'm reminded of the four winds of the ancient Greeks: Boreas(North)—Zephryous(West)—Eurus (East)—Notos(South). These were Gods. As a group they were called the ANEMOI. Yes, 'n' I'll change that to ANEMOION; that holistic grasp/hug/hold/songs of these forces of the Earth. Alas, a name for the ever-increasing winds, ever-dominating winds of climate change. Somewhere in there that M stands for Maria's blowing our love back to us.

With this ANEMOION in mind as an all-encompassing wind in our face, tossing our hair, making us hold on to a tree and one another, I recall these lines from my "Saddled On Memory" of 2012:

> Saddled on Memory we stride the wind,
> Thundering hooves bounce us clung to the mane.
> Borne by Memory to begin again.
> Magnificent the ride on dawn's whirlwind,
> Leaping through sunsets across the moon's wane;
> Saddled on Memory we stride the wind.
> Forgetting's easy in the racing wind,
> And stumbles in the stretch can make us lame.
> Saddled on Memory we stride the wind,
> Borne by Memory to begin again.

So many have lost their treasured memories in homes, and lives consumed by fire and shattered by winds. They must feel the "spirit-stay" of memories inside their consciousness and that "holding" will to begin again. So much talk of a "new normal" – our never returning to blessings of yesterday. Yet, we must saddle on our memory to stride the howling winds of tomorrow's changes. Yes, 'n' there'll be new songs to sing….along with the oldies. In so many ways we are all candles in the wind calling on Maria for our loves; with the winds blowing us down-around: yet, we feel the lift, the memory, the spiritual power of the heroic wind beneath our wings. ---- Suddenly, after writing this, I had the vision of a horse and eagle. Oh -- to have an image of them together at this point. So, I went to the internet. WOW! WOW! Many have been way ahead of me. Many many images of them together, just as I imagined. What's more! A 1990's song/production by John Denver (I never knew of it) – EAGLES AND HORSES, with these lyrics throughout the song:

> I had a vison of eagles and horses
> High on a ridge in a race with the wind
> Going higher and higher and faster and faster
> On eagles and horses I'm flying again!

O! POIOEMA of the ANEMOION! O! Candle in the Wind! O! GOTMOL!

Saddled on Memory we fly the ANSWER. Belongsongs lifting our wings!

SOMEWHERE DEEP IN THE HIDDEN DOWN

Where winds blow not in the channels
      Nor gust at the peaks. Somewhere
In the hidden down a sparked blooding in silence flows,
Vein-pulsed in the mire of dark, exquisite chemistries,
      Toned though organ reciprocities,
      Synapses fired for symphonic chordalities. . . .
Exhaled from something mired deep in the hidden down –
It's flowing percussion to be a voice in the wilderness,
      Where winds blow hard in the songsome-songdone vistas,
      Cascading the valleys with time's erosions
      Through extremities and lips murmured of dreams,
Music, and logos words aburst from hopeful seams,
Sewn and sown somewhere deep in the hidden down
      Where capillaries longing for choruses and soliloquies,
      Crest to suffers-of-light and airy alchemic rustings.
Now, inhales of turbulence to the flesh of the deep hidden down,
Erupting a voice to sound the wild-waters flowing . . . .
All's wild caught, now, in surface-heaves of the deeper silence flowing,
      A rising "thar-she-blows" at the sun-high peaks gusting,
      Bucking on the to-and-fro of the channeled winds blowing:
Tangoed in the bivalve pranayama of the windless into the wind,
Glowingly exhaled in the caught and release gusts of the inhale wind
      Deep into the breathlessness . . . .

Before the hidden down . . . . beyond the hidden down.

[The Hidden-Down is our biological ensemble in full harmonic hold. (Recall the Interstitium!) It seeks expressive release to join the Hold of existence. An aroused reciprocity sought beyond the hidden-down to join the en-choiring of the world. Like a whale jumping from the sea into the sunlight. A mind joining the eagle in flight, the horse in gallop: wind for wings, ground for hooves: mind's for thoughts and lungs for breath. The Hidden Down – Up and About! Implied here is my sense that breathing as inhalation and exhalation --- is fundamentally a dynamic of how the universe functions. I've no mathematics for this or savants to quote. Seems very much connected to consciousness and our "holding" capability – therefore a vibrating thought pattern that won't go away. Surely, this is in the context of the anthropic principle on a creaturely-earthly scale: the body's interior's reciprocity with the exteriors of Earth. Just found a term for it: SYMPATHOMIMETIC. While it refers to outside synthetic medicines which mirror the wellness "fight" within. This reflects a major theme in my book SYMPATHIES and is carried forward with GOTMOL's THE HOLD and BELONGSONG, which are sympathetic mirrorings of true holdings from both realms of human and world. Such BONDHOLDCOVENANTS (BOHOCO's) show the "hidden" magic of THE HOLD. — What holds a star holds a backyard fire.]

HEADS UP! - HOLD ON! – LOOK OUT!

Now there's a threesome for you. Any grasp of a meaning of life will have experiences from these perspectives built in. One could call them a holistic holding pattern as one engages the world with one's life in every circumstance. Of course, these are all active in the concepts of the HEAD as discussed above. Right now, the issue is the main issue of THE HOLD as it is the permanent reality in existence and therefore in our minds also. In brief, existences, living things, and consciousness awareness persist because they hold together.

Let's look, again, at the terms I've incorporated in HEAD:
Holistoions Evolutionary Aligned Destiny as Hold Everything And Dance!

These are easy to comprehend because they are so everyday GUT&TOE2HEAD real. Every era has this natural awareness – as real. Existences exist because they are of a belongingness that holds and evolves to align with their environment and therefore manifest a destiny that holds. Cardinals keep producing Cardinals. It's the whatever is going on making masses-- stars and starfish, planets and people, galaxies and geographies – hold together to be what they are. Humans are special in this enterprise because we are conscious observers of everything else, which is the observed. I'll have to say more about this as this writing evolves, but note now that my continuing emphasis on the OiO of the SYNTANGOION – contains graphically the two Os of Observer and Observed – as it represents all other reciprocillation of polarities and the third reality they create, which carries, as offspring, the "holding pattern" of I Am That I Am of both worlds. (That TANGO cosmic partner's dance.) Alas,we are the measurers of the measurable; once we say it's 4 it is that. If we see it as both particle and wave – it (and both) is as we see it. It's the Hold-On between Heads-Up and Look-Out! Does that mean the "hold" of "consciousness" is created by this interplay? Maybe! Maybe Not! We've a few hurdles before that comes to signature our highest-hurdle jump. [Note: Einstein's E=mc2 can be read – Existence Equals Mass Times Consciousness Squared. It holds that triune grasp as does the Syntangoion. Lucky You, I'm not a trained mathematician or I'd flourish many a formula of elegance(?)!]

First, I need to quote from F. Capra's THE TAO OF PHYSICS. This is a difficult selection – so much is relevant. I just returned to this book, feeling/remembering it spoke to me about "my world" in many ways. Quite possible my sensing of THE HOLD got an early TAO inspiration there. One thinks so, hold as flow/flow as hold, with these ideas:

"The age-old tradition of explaining complex structures by breaking them down into simpler constituents is so deeply ingrained in Western thought that the search for these basic components is still going on. --- There is, however, a radically different school of thought in particle physics which starts from the idea that nature cannot be reduced to fundamental particles, such as elementary particles or fundamental fields. It has to be understood entirely through its self-consistency, with its components being consistent with one another and themselves. . . .In the new world-view, the universe is seen as a dynamic web of interrelated events. None of the properties of any part of the web is fundamental; they all follow from the properties of the other parts, and the overall consistency of their mutual interrelations determines the structure of the entire web." (pp. 315-316)

This is enough, in essence, to show the stirrings of THE HOLD and the HEAD. And, true to his title he wrote this to further the concept:

"For the Taoist sages, all phenomena in the world were part of the Cosmic Way –the Tao—and the laws followed by the Tao were not laid down by any divine lawgiver, but were inherent in its nature. Thus we read in the Tao Te Ching:

> Man follows the laws of the earth;
> Earth follows the laws of heaven;
> Heaven follows the laws of Tao;
> Tao follows the laws of its intrinsic nature." (p.319)

Capra concluded this book discussing David Bohm and his concepts of "implicate Order" and "Holomovement." This was to give emphasis to a dynamic unity rather than structures of objects. "According to Bohm, space and time emerge as forms flowing out of the holomovement; they, too, are enfolded in its order." --- And the book is pretty much summed by this at the conclusion:

"To understand the implicate order, Bohm has found it necessary to regard consciousness as an essential feature of the holomovement and to take it in to account explicitly in his theory. He sees mind and matter as being interdependent and correlated, but not causally connected. They are mutually enfolding projections of a higher reality which is neither matter or consciousness." (p. 353)

Wikipedia has a good article on HOLOMOVEMENT as an "undivided wholeness" with a "universal flux" ever in the "state of becoming." From Bohm's "Wholeness and the Implicate Order" (1980) this end of book quote:

"Our overall approach has thus brought together questions of the nature of the cosmos, of matter in general, of life, and of consciousness. All of these have considered to be projections of a common ground. This we may call the ground of all that is." (p.212) Alas, HOLOCOHO -- Holistic Covenantal Holding.

These quotes are to give dimension and explanation of my calling this "higher reality" of "the ground of all that is" – THE HOLD and HOLISTOIONS. And conceiving such as a state of becoming that makes a giraffe as a galaxy: in other words, as each became as they are by becoming and holding: a common ground it is. As I am writing this little book, I just became aware – Facebook Advertising – of an author and concept I hadn't heard of before. The new release book is "The Grand Biocentric Design – How Life Creates Reality" – authors Lanza, Pavsic, and Berman. In time, I will read this book as I, someday, further my research on "consciousness." The main theme of these scientists seems to be this: biological "consciousness" is the primary means of our perception: *we make the world appear as it is.* (I'm saying the contrary.) From excerpts I've read there seems to a direct connection to Bohn-Capra and my concepts as described here. But these authors seem to take consciousness to realms beyond Holomovement and The Hold. So, another time for the "bio" of this Toe-Gut-Head—the BOD: Bard-Ovate-Druid ! This from "Sympathies":

PROPHET – Distantly, I do see a time when consciousness,
this "home of the brave," planet-patriotism,
will be uploaded on nonbiological conductors
on intergalactic flights. Contact! Transmission
shared with alien processors in deep, deep space.
Consciousnesses exchanged: down-loaded cool and bright.
as bioluminescence turns on the light.
If we don't mess-up the planet's first flight,
we'll know more of otherness, nothingness, and earthiness then,
and of webbed feet surfing cool in galaxial curls.
Close encounters of any kind, if ever,
would win with a John William's score;
the heartstrings of T's and ET's
phoning home to talk about it;
get on the monitor and wave a "Hi, Mom!"
> *"How Are Things In Glocca Morra?*
> *Is That Little Brook Still Leaping There?*
> *Does It Still Run Down To Donny-Cove?*
> *Through Killybegs, Kilkerry And Kildare?*

Remember, I'm not a scientist or professor of anything. I'm a self-trained-self-strained POET. I have paid close attention to this life of mine and environs and others where my role has been played… and still is. So this GOTMOL is my attempt at this moment in time to sing, with meaning, the song of my very own self as gracenote as it plays into the major composition of life. Actually, my book SYMPATHIES was about this concept in so many ways. A good recall is this phrase from Leibnitz (p. 289-290):-- *harmonia praestabilia*, which refers to a pre-established harmony that works in the belongingness of things to become what they should/could be. Call this the HARP. Whether it plays by some divinity or just a natural affinity – is the never-ending query. For me, it seems more a natural affinity – as it is the "holding" that patterns existences to live a harmonic HOLD which holds. My house, my world as yours, is full of things which have become what they are because they found what fits. And a lot of human creativity has had its play in what has been made by our own hands and brains using available HARP-HOLDS such a water, sunshine, trees and soil… and our creaturely selves. Sure enough, our spirituality, sense of purpose, creativity, and daily meaning --- come from this reality pervasive in all existence. That reality – HA-HO! in brief, is an *acheiropoieton*: a reality like our planet – not made by human hands but in our hands as is the oak tree. We use the quintessential Hold that molds us to mold our lives and things to Hold.

It is this HEAD-HA-HO! at work, beyond the farms, that has become the internet, massive telescopes, rockets, iPhones, computers, drones, guns, ships, and ------- robots. Put this 3H world together in a human mimicking robot and, for some scientists like Ray Kurzweil, you can write a book called "The Age of Spiritual Machines" – wherein machines can talk to machines with much more intelligence and advanced HEAD-HA-HO! than humans can muster. Kurzweil writes: ". . . that once the evolution of life-forms sets in, the emergence of a species that creates technology is inevitable. The evolution of the technology is then a continuation by other means of the evolution that gave rise to the technology-creating species in the first place."(p.255) Then you have the "age of computation" evolving and the merger of human and computer taking-off in all kinds of ways --- some very good and some very bad. We are learning how to manage HEADS UP!-HOLD-ON!-LOOK-OUT! -- in this newly evolved world that's a marriage of humans and technology. Ahh! A *menage a trois!* Eartharian climate issues join-in. Kurzweil's world is one of evolving intelligence, wherein eventually machine intelligence with surpass human intelligence. The biocentric view makes consciousness pervasive. Define each howsoever, the HEAD-HA-HO-HOLOCOHO! plays the same music. Virtue as valid valiant voiced virtuosity.

Personally, I don't think machines will ever "feel" or "love" being held. Will they get aroused on the dance floor? Have sex? Offspring? Congestion? Pain? Wake-up in the middle of the night with a brilliant thought? As I write there is much ado about a COVID-19 vaccine before year's end. Whatever the time table – the "what holds process" is underway to find what "holds together" as that works to be "held" in our bodies. So much is happening in the bio-tech world that which works so intimately with how our bodies function. In my book SYMPATHIES I explored these issue and all in this writing under the theme of "the en-choiring of sympathies." Getting the right voices together and giving them the song they best can sing. The word "gracings" refers to that finding the right song to sing…and knowing it is right. Howsoever reality got so programmed is difficult to comprehend. Still, it manifests the meaning of life in us as we find our song and can dance with realities that hold true for us and by which we feel "truly held" and firmly in place.This is not difficult to comprehend in our daily lives. We are engaged in holding patterns every moment.

It is our nature to pursue purpose, beauty, truth, love, family, intuition, creativity, etc., etc. These are holdings. Herbert Read in his book THE MEANING OF ART – works it all down to THE WILL TO FORM. Art is a function of our MEANING OF LIFE. Namely, to find, create, experience the forms of existence that hold us securely—belongingly-- in place. Memories and Goals alive! And, O! – the persistent challenge of those FORMS UNKNOWN. Ahh! Humanity's ultimate grace is to song its belonging belongsong!

HUG2BE

HUMANITY'S ULTIMATE GRACE TO BELONG

WHAT IS THIS QUINTESSENCE OF DUST?

What a piece of work is man! How noble in reason. How infinite in faculties! In form and moving, how express and admirable! In action how like an angel! In apprehension, how like a god! The beauty of the world! The parqgon of animals! And yet, to me, what is this quintessence of dust?

Shakespeare's Hamlet

Ah! A Consciousness of Belonging with a Belonging Consciousness – which sings with A Death in Life that's A Life in Death and manages many a breath-held tonal soundings that harmonize with the surround to from a choir of sympathies that sing and dance as HOLISTOIONS of the SYNTANGOION.

See, how easy that was to answer? Our To Be — is to become, to be held, and to belong: to cause… because. The quintessence that "holds-forms-enchoirs" it all is our belongsong. – In my lifetime, I've sung with five different choirs. From my experience, I would require "choir" in every high school curriculum. Those with choral belongingness experience are not the sources of violence. Keats sang – "Beauty is truth, truth beauty," --- that is all Ye know on earth, and all ye need to know." Alas, this was a "belongsong," but Keats forgot the "belonging" twixt beauty and truth. An Ode is such a song. A Grecian Urn is such a song of belonging. Behold! I stand twixt the oak tree and the formulae of science, holding an urn that sings my belonging and manifests my being home--- rather than homeless. I concluded my Villanelle "We Long To Belong And Sing To Say So" with this:

> *Travelling in time we go as we must go!*
> *Never footsore of authenticity.*
> *We long to belong and sing to say so.*
> *Every trail's to home that sings the way so.*

The choral power of that "authenticity" is our home-found-belongingness. It is this which rings true within the reciprocillations of truth&beauty//life&death and all the other dialogic polarities, complexities, and stirrings of our everyday world. It is that which makes us sing-dance-compose our belongsong. Suicide, depression: lives of violence are due to losses of holds of authenticity and belonging. Yes, the ever-flow "gracions" of GOTMOL are the true and beautiful belongingnesses of being at home. In my last words to my dying Marilyn, I told her, as she asked, that she would always have a home: her paintings, photos, personal treasures – would all still HOLD their belongsong life ever at home and with her family. With *"Glistenings,"* I shared her song with the world. This from SYMPATHIES:

O! P O E M ! --- PEACE ON EARTH MUSIC!

Like oracles, orisons, and deep AUMs,
Music rises through the soles of our feet,
Soars like angels butterflied from the land,
Their wings the flowing waters, wind-song tones
Whipping blooms from trees to fly with the bees;
Flutterflybyes' strobe-winds tune strings and reeds;
Earth's orchestral, a play, an opera,
An oratorium with brassability:
Four seasons, bowing as a string quartet,
Chords from crescendos to catastrophes –
Sound off the rocks, the rills, the sensuals.
We are the composers with the primal vibes –
The players, singers, dancers and the choir.
Profound music fills profound mystery.
The hills are alive with its do-re-me.
Earth's the Performance Hall ---- Planet Center.
Like whales, dolphins and swans – we have our song.
To Choir or not to Choir's an answered quest,
As we honk-soar with the wild gander's flight,
Feel the *mysterium tremendum's* might:
Conduct the chorus the whole world sings –
And answer to each call the earthtone rings.
Then.......A new era of Choral Masterworks
Is ready to change the sound of the world.
Time to launch a World Peace Choir IPO:
Songs performed every audience can sing.
I seek the wands to wave the magic home.
Gather the singers like Cardinals to Rome:
Form them in choirs at every Peace Summit!
The UN needs a Choir! Composers to Song it!

THE H A L L E H O L D Y O U C H O R U S ! ! !

RECOMPOSING THE ORPHEUS BELONGSONG

This is the famous relief image of Hermes-Eurydice-Orpheus in the Museo Nazionale, Naples. Orpheus and Eurydice are having their last "touching" moment of belonging before Hermes escorts her back to Hades and Orpheus returns to Earth alone. Eurydice is dead and can't be brought back to earthly life by Orpheus as in the first tales of the myth. Or, the relief shows the opposite – that Orpheus is getting Eurydice delivered to him by Hermes to take back to the living. Orpheus was an "original-primal" poet-musician character whose singing and playing of the lyre resonated with the trees, rocks, animals and all of nature. And it was this power of performance that got him into Hades place of the dead and then managed her release to go back with Orpheus. [My two favorite books for all this story-history are – Charles Segal's ORPHEUS: The Myth of the Poet – and – M. Owen Lee's VIRGIL AS ORPHEUS: A Study of the Georgics.]

But, along comes Virgil and his Georgics around 29 BCE – some 400 years after this relief by an unknown creator came to be: but, which it is thought Virgil had seen.) Virgil's is the first written accounting of this story. He made Orpheus disregard Hade's (Pluto's) request that he not look back for her as she was following him back to the world of the living or he would lose her forever. Virgil just said Orpheus forgot for a moment or was moved by passion. Thinking perhaps as he reached the sunlight of the real world she should be there at that moment of "belonging." Whatever. Writers/composers have since in many ways played on that "passion" as sexual-romance need and motivation for such. Indeed, that an overly needful weakness moved his head. She was lost. Orpheus came back with no further interest in women. Thus, the Dionysiac Bacchantes were appalled that he was both defeated by death and lost his interest in women --and tore him apart. Apollo took his Lyre and put his ever-singing head in a cave: which sings-cries still through the songs of the Nightingales.

So, this is a story of poetry, music, our place in nature – dealing with the reality of death. In my view, Orpheus looked back because Eurydice called out to him, in his consciousness of belonging, that Hades was not going to let her go. The word "passion" calls up many pursuits of purposeful intent. When the suddenness of the unchangeable fact of death screams its inevitability into your soul – you cannot help but look back to hold on to all you can still grasp of that "presence" of your belonging. And what killed Orpheus was a society not ready to live with death's inevitability and the quest or peace on earth -- and that our songs and poetries couldn't change that. That struggle is still going on with religions and beliefs, namely, that we pass-on to another world were Orpheus will be with Eurydice again when he, too, dies. So many, still sing the song that "God needed another Angel."

Virgil knew he was living/writing at a pivotal moment in history. Wars and death were everywhere. His best friend died. (The poet-soldier, Gallos.) Eurydice symbolized Gallo's loss to Virgil as some interpret. Octavian was in charge – of either advancing slaughter or advancing peace. Whatever, the reality of death is a fact. We can't bring them back. And we can't help but look back. Much of our belongsong is the belonging of our memory. And, Virgil stressed in his Georgics (supposedly reading them for four days to Octavian), our belongingness to nature, agriculture, and the fields. He hopes for peace and his success in so convincing Octavian. But, M. Owen Lee reads Virgil as follows:

"Virgil hopes that, if we see his meaning (*sua si bona norint*, 2.458), we will find happiness and peace (*fortunatus et ille deos qui novit agrestis*, 2.493). But he has the feeling, too that, through no fault of his own, he may fail in his mission (*has ne possim naturae accedere partis*, 2.483). Perhaps this is why he changed the story of Orpheus and had the mythic poet fail in his mission." (p. 40)

There is always with the artist a sense of "failure" to reconcile death with a sense of the eternal in art: the spirit and matter conundrum. Segal said this regarding the figure of Orpheus in his discussion of Rilke:

"Orpheus' power of song embodies the power of language to impose form on the formless through meaning and classification. In him song-poetry – can also view and hold the fleeting moment in stable cohesion and fixity. . . .His (Rilke's) Orpheus is a symbol of process rather than fixity, a locus where irreconcilable, and therefore tragic, oppositions meet. The power of language that he symbolizes is not merely a language as magical persuasion but language reaching toward transcendence while yet not denying its ground in the time, death, and suffering of language users, mortals." (p. 126-127)

"Fixity" is not a word-same as "holding." Even the "held" in the holding is not fixity. "Belonging," rather magically one might say, is the holding pattern of process. Another word for it is "memory," which is ever a "holding process." Silence and meditation the same. M. Owen Lee comments on Virgil's Georgics:

". . .the perceptible things in the Georgics suggest some non-quite-perceptible dimension that, if grasped, would explain the entire poem. One of the mythic figures Virgil introduces at the end of the poem is wise old Proteus, who knows past, present, and future, but must be grasped and held fast if he is to reveal his secrets. The Georgics itself is, from first to last, a protean poem." (p.40)

Segal and Lee are both vibrantly alive within the full Orphic-Protean grasp of mortal/immortal, immanent/transcendent, transient/eternal - life in death//death in life: constant reciprocillations of time/eternity - process and fixity. (Recall the – SYNTANGOION!) We are a mix of Orpheus and

Proteus: Orpheus is Proteus and Proteus is Orpheus. We keep writing songs and poetries that hold us in the held of belonging: from the HOLD come new songs. We can run because our feet hold fast to the ground. Segal concludes as follows:

"How will this myth continue its life in the poems of generations to come? I can only point to what it has meant over the past twenty-five-hundred years of Western civilization that I have so briefly summarized. It offers the creative artist the power to feel his art as a magic that touches the sympathetic chords in all of nature and puts him in touch with the thrill of pure life, pure Being. They myth of Orpheus is the myth of the ultimate seriousness of art. It is the myth of total engagement with love, beauty, and the order and harmony of nature – all under the sign of death. It is the myth of the artist's magic, of his courage for the dark, desperate plunge into the depths of the heart, and of the world, and of his hope and need to return and tell the rest of us of his journey." (p.198)

All do not write and compose/construct as poets, artists, and musicians or philosophers. Yet, all live (to live beyond death) for the held of the hold of their Time's Eternal Now, belonging. Indeed, happiest are those who know their belongsong -- the tune, lyrics, instruments – it's pauses and progressions: it's home. Orpheus composes and sings in the midst of death and dying of the SHOALS OF WONTSUNODI – those Shining Holds of Angelic Legacies of Wonders That Should Not Die. Such are "gracings" of the meaning of life. To me, "Grace" embodies/enchoirs/ennobles the wholesome feel/knowledge of being "held" by what holds and the tones of the belongsong we sing. Grace is, perhaps, such as Virgil saw in the human progeny potential of a some yet to be born child who would bring peace to the world. What a paradigm shift: real persons to replace the mythos of the gods. Now the POEM—Peace On Earth Music: POETS Passage Owl's Epiphanic Tang. HUG2BE Humanity's Ultimate Grace To Belong/Beheld/Behold/Become. HUGS-OF-COHO at HOME TOKHOLITU: Humanity's Universal Global Summons of Covenantal Holding at Humanity's Own Mother Earth: The Only Known Home Of Life In The Universe.

Ah, the Ark of the Covenant. It possessed a different kind of power over nature than Orpheus with his singing and strumming. It was a physical power to part the seas and defeat the enemies. It carried the power of JAH. One of the first trinities is the two angels beholding that presence between them. It symbolized/carried the power of the supreme deity, who could cause all sorts of problems for those who did not Covenant with HIM. The Arc no longer exists, but the ever-present need to covenant with peoples and the earth is ever-so evident. The SHOALS of WONTSUNODI preside over that.

Orpheus, too, is gone – but his artistic connect/alignment with the natural world is an always been-never-ending covenant. That's a winner even though he failed to overcome death. Then came Christianity with its dogma that Jesus conquered death and is the portal for all to do so. Well that's a belief system for those who want to so believe, but it has no fact in reality. The Arc is gone. Jesus is gone. Eurydice and Orpheus are gone. But the courage in looking back (think Big Bang, how science works, and, in general, learning from the past), shows how life's trinities, and the Protean-Covenantal "holding of the held" have prevailed as necessary and quintessentially so. We turn back, full stature, and look at Death face-to-face. So it is we have looked back to envision the Big Bang: are able to plot the character of the universe, wherein, it seems, everything eventually dies. --Just as Orpheus has stepped into the sunlight of the real world – he hears:

> E ----ORPHEUS! ORPHEUS!
> Look at me! Pluto has deceived you!
> I cannot return to life with you.
> I'm calling you to sing a new song with me.
> Look at me! Let us see what holds to sing.
> O ----EURYDICE! EURYDICE!
> What song to sing?
> If I look back, I lose you forever.
> How can I sing with you?
> E ----Memory! Memory!
> You can look back and see me still: Hold me still!
> You have not lost "hold" of me.
> And though death take me – I know
> I'll be held in all songs you sing! Tomorrow!&Tomorrow!
> O ---- I'm looking back, now.
> I see you "holding" in my mind.
> You are not there. O the agony!
> You're gone, but singing within me!
> I wail and cry the emptiness. Where did you go!!!
> E ---- Hold me! Caress Me! Embrace Me!
> I am yours for as long as you can hold me
> O ----Ah! the new songs I'll must sing now.
> Songs that never lose the embrace or
> Your hold of memory. Our song sung till the end of time.
> E - Our Eternal Now Hold of Belongsong wonders that should not die.
> O - I Embrace You! I Hold your hand in the palm of my mind!
>   The sun is shining! Come! Hold-On with Me! We're going home!

The Tsunami of death has always crashed on the loveliest of humanity's shores and homeland. It rises higher today as the vulnerabilities and changes on our planet Earth are increasingly present and precarious. We are ever looking into the face/fact of death. No GOTMOL can avoid it and must absorb it as the air we breathe. The "G" is for living's existential graces – not for God. God is but a concept, seems to me, that arises from the natural "hold" of things as I've tried to describe it. Call it the COHO of OTCITBYBELTER – Covenantal Holdings of Things Coming Into Themselves By Belonging Together. All such events have this as their belongsong – be they trees, bees, or people. Consciousness as we know it is a belonging together. . . with that added extra of a belonging beyond belonging. Yes, I did have a discussion, all too briefly, years ago with Tillich about his concept of "God beyond God." That search never ends: our longing to belong beyond death is a wish-wish that'll never wash-wash away. But, immortality is a wish/fantasy with no confirmed content. We agreed – the quest would ever-continue its reach for that higher ground.

One of the gracings of the COHO is our sense of time. Holding patterns have changes --- as one thing leads to another. There are intervals. We have timed those intervals in many ways, But the measurements of the holding and releasing of events are ours. We are now able to take our measurement skills to the universe as we can see/read it through our telescopes and theories. Brian Greene's new book is entitled "Until The End Of Time." Carlo Rovelli's is "The Order of Time." Scientists have seen an inflationary universe and that along with all else witnessed so far – there is the conclusion that all this existence will (in time…as we know it) fizzle-out to cinders that crumble into dust that dissipates into some form of nothingness. Time's Up! Alas, by our sense of time – that is billions of billions of billions of years away. And we and earth will have vanished many billions of years before that. Time, as conceived, is, after all, a holding/unfolding pattern.

Hey! Hey! There may be a something GOD beyond-before all of this. Hey! Maybe, in time, the great exhalation will suddenly do an inhalation and all will crunch back to start all over again with a Big Bang Being Breath Blast. Actually, I think a cyclical universe based on a breathing in and out and holding sequence is the most interesting. But as yet no TOE GUT as we scratch our HEAD and hold it high. Sigh! Somethings about it all rings of an eternity where our sense of time is meaningless. Ah! Time beyond Time! Hey! With the likes of Greene and Rovelli -- I'll tackle that another time. I'll be surprised if they can convince me the universe knows what time it is.

In the meantime, we and our planet live our belong in what holds to be held in the belong of our beholdings. -- Words! Unavoidably! Poetries and Songs!! Reasons & Purposes to hold because and before we fold! Gracenotes to enfold/enchoir their belong into the flowing/playing symphony. The best bet in this ever-shuffling/ever-dealing game of life is our belongsong. This is why families, religion, churches, societies, groups (bars- restaurants-theater) are significant: they are where humans belong (hold-held-hugged) and from that belonging we sing/write/dance our belongsong. Memory is a belonging with its own kind of belongsong. Perhaps the one word that holds it all is EMBRACE – which rhymes, of course, with GRACE. [And ACE!]

HOLD YOUR ACES -- ACE YOUR HOLDS

MEANING IN LIFE -- LIFE IN MEANING

GRACE YOUR TIME -- TIME YOUR GRACE

HOLD YOUR HUG -- HUG YOUR HOLD

SYNC YOUR DANCE -- DANCE YOUR SYNC

FORM FOLLOWS FUNCTION -- FUNCTION FOLLOWS FORM

MIND SPIRITS BODY -- BODY SPIRITS MIND

CONSCIOUSNESS BEHOLDS BELONGING
BELONGING BEHOLDS CONSCIOUSNESS

BRAIN EMBODIES MIND -- MIND EMBODIES BRAIN, ETC.

"Nothing in the world is single. All things by a law divine
In one another's being mingle." -- Shelley

Geologists have a way of talking about mountain ranges. Some are stable, some rise, and some decrease. Those that hold in place possess an "equilibrium" between "uplift" and "erosion." This defines a "holding pattern" relevant to all living things. -- Behold The Hold! Source of the "divinities," the "law divine," the "soul," and Loves of Being Held. The Radiance of Immanence. Dawn on the Lawn. Memory! "Daylight! I must think of the sunrise. I must think of a new day – and I mustn't give in." In the mingle's a tingle that gives us our tangle. An Equilibrium with Peaks! O! Memories of Maslow's "Peak Experiences" of personal fulfillment.

O! Poetries Of Epiphanic Tang.

ACE IN THE HOLD

A personal note! Some months ago, I sent a brief essay to the UU World magazine that was completely ignored. The gist of it was as stated on my website: I'm changing my professional title of Reverend to Covenend – Cove O'Kelly verses Rev O'Kelly. Since the Rev title is the usage of Christianity and inclusive of all far-right Evangelicals, with whom I am a liberal-progressive-humanistic contrast totally, I refuse to be a hypocrite – indeed – refuse to proclaim a falsity to the world or myself. I am not a minister of the Christian Gospel, howsoever interpreted, and cannot/should not use a title that doesn't apply to me and my sense of life's meaning and purposeful fulfillment. I'm not "really" a "minister of religion," where the phrase "people of faith" engenders confusion. I was, however, a "Minister" of reverence, covenant, spirituality – and reason. The word "reverence" as in "reverence for life," is, of course, maintained and rhymes/syncs/thinks naturally with "covenance." This is controversial, of course. No offers, yet, to debate the issue. I've no guru glams to internet a movement. I document it as my "existential integrity." My embrace-gracings-belongsong are not of a dogmatic, biblical based religious tradition. Church, Temple, Synagogue, Shrine, Altar . . . whatever. . .are gathering places for those who are so gathered by their belief in Life After Death and some Eternity for their continuance. I see only this Life before Death. I covenant with the world-earth-peoples-promises-potential, etc. of this life. Trying to hold what holds best in the holdings and "thresholdings" of this life. AH! The Embrace of Grace in this ACE of a Place. I'll "covenantally embrace"(COVE) with that. The ACE of HOLDS in this engaging shuffle/dealing/gaming life is our *Astonishing Covenantal Embrace*. That I Trust! Behold! See ACE in *Grace-Embrace-Face-Place-Peace-Trace-Race!* And keep up the PACE of compassion, family, love, accomplishment, fulfillment, happiness, prosperity, truth, beauty, etc, as such (super) natural gracings are ever-in-resonance to structure our belongsong's harmonic hold midst challenges of dissonance.

Always, writing such, I hear calls from the mysterium tremendum fascinans of the complexio oppositorum of something/nothing – meaning each implies the other ("spooky action at a distance") for each to be their own manifestation – and have a relationship that reciprocally holds – such that a third (that "tertium quid" as some "tertium comparationis," or, in other words "contraria sunt complementia") – which is, rather miraculously, THE HOLD that manifests to keep all dynamically united midst the in-and-out of symmetries. (SYNTANGOION's "I" symbolizes this. This one sentence, too.)

Well, this should not be too difficult to comprehend. There is no life without death and no death without life. No inhalation without exhalation. No creation without destruction. No predation without procreation. And, in the reciprocal interplay of these there arises oak trees, baboons and us. No beast without beauty. No horror without honorable. So! So! So! It goes! -- And, Oh!, to say with a holding-feel-of-truth – IN THE HOLD I TRUST, which gives us our us and an I for an I. I've called it the ACE IN THE HOLD: that Astonishing Covenantal Embrace that makes trees, racoons, finches and species all. I took the word "astonishing" from the book QUANTUM PHYSICS FOR POETS, by Lederman and Hill (Prometheus Books, 2011), assuming much scientific data proceeding – some I understood:

"So the exchanged wave function can either be 'symmetrical,' that is +1, times the original one, or else it can be 'anti-symmetrical', or -1 times the original one. Either as is allowed, in principle, because we can measure only the probabilities (the squares of wave functions). – In fact, quantum mechanics allows both possibilities, so nature finds a way to offer both possibilities, and the result is astonishing." (p. 294)

[THE HOLD is the "result."]

[Another author, Stephen Earl Robbins, in his book TIME AND MEMORY: A Primer on the scientific mysticism of consciousness (private publication), introduces his book with the following, which uses different language to report the same astonishment:

"This will be a focus on the *everyday* mysticism of experience – "Channel Normal" if you will – and the reasons why it is so. Our everyday perception of the coffee cup is as mystical as a Zen enlightenment. It is not for nothing that the Buddha said, "Samsara *is* Nirvana. -p- Samsara – the world of everyday objects, of coffee cups and spoons – is mystical. This is simply not understood, either by non-mystics or by science. We will be seeing how mystical our Channel Normal really is, how far we are from robotic machines, and we will be getting glimpses of potentials we actually hold as beings, far beyond the limited and limiting conceptions of the machine model of mind." (p. xiii)]

That "Channel Normal" ("we actually hold") is that cup, that tree – that thought and breath I hold consciously. The Hold is in everything. The term "mysticism" works for some. I prefer "spiritual," which includes it. I so refer to it to my writings as POANSWER --- Poetries of a New Spirituality We Are. New – because of the advancement of the sciences and the global inclusiveness created by climate change crises, contagions, and internet, technical connections (HOLDS) as never before. Many no longer believe in the traditional religions. All concepts of "The New Being" --- front and center! The Deal is On! Place your bet on the ACES IN THE HOLD.

Ahh! Photo of me with a tree that beckoned its behold just outside the Blarney-Stone Castle in May 2019. Good enough to image our natural holding poetries for this little missive of GOTMOL. Just another GOTMOL one might say. Cove O'Kelly on location! Who needs a Blarney-Stone? I've Blarney Barks/Branches & Blooms in my backyard

BEHOLD! THE TREE OF LIFE! STRUCTURE OF THE HOLD!

Here's another "today" from science of the GOTMOL workings of THE HOLD. A company in CA, Newlight Technologies, has created a biodegradable product to replace plastic. Seems our oceans are full of microorganisms that feed on methane and carbon dioxide and producing from that feeding a natural polymer (pure white power) that can be shaped and molded like plastic. In brief, this is air and greenhouse gases dissolved in water with its mircoorganisms. Such are EFI's – Environmentally Friendly Innovations. But Newlight's discovery and process is a contemporary example *par excellence* of how THE HOLD works with things coming into themselves by belonging together. VOILA!

Here's another Eagle song –"On Eagle's Wings," by Michael Jongas (Priest). This is the choral refrain used five times: *And He will raise you upon eagle wings – Bear you on the breath of dawn – Make you to shine like the sun – And hold you in the palm of His hand.* Very fine poetry. (Music I don't know.) The "hold" of earth's realities (eagle, breath, dawn, sun, shining, "palm of…hand") are to me THE HOLD from which arises concepts of Lord-His-He as the Holder. Behold earth's Tree of Life's "hold" of memory & praise.

[Speaking of Blarney, with the Fairy Folk all about – I offer this bit of mythos/mystery for "thought" in GOTMOL. This: Physicists talk of annihilations of plus and minus polarities and the consequent dilemma of where does matter (something existing) come from if all is annihilated? Answer: the event of Nothing & Something is holistically itself a "Something." Therefore, Something – existence – will always be. Even annihilation events are SOMETHING – and that constitutes a "holding pattern" called THE HOLD. Alas, this could be but a poet's blarney, but I bet there's an elegant formula for it. Recall the poetries/polarities of the quintessence of THE HOLD above on page 15.

THE BELONGSONG-DEATHSONG OF THE GOTMOL

Having employed songs variously in this address, I feel I should introduce this concluding section with a song that sings of so much I've tried to say about what graces the meaning of life with a truthful hold. I have chosen Charles Kingsley's poem/song THE SANDS OF DEE in its entirety:

> O Mary, go and call the cattle home,
>   And call the cattle home,
>   And call the cattle home,
>   Across the sands of Dee.
> The western wind was wild and dank with foam,
>   And all alone went she.
>
> The western tide crept up along the sand,
>   And o'er and o'er the sand,
>   And round and round the sand,
>   As far as eye could see.
> The rolling mist came down and hid the land:
>   And never home came she.
>
> Oh! Is it weed, or fish, or floating hair –
>   A tress of golden hair,
>   A drowned maiden's hair
>   Above the nets at sea?
> Was never salmon yet that shone so fair
>   Among the stakes on Dee.
>
> They rowed her in across the rolling foam,
>   The cruel crawling foam,
>   The cruel hungry foam,
>   To her grave beside the sea:
> But still the boatmen hear her call the cattle home
>   Across the sands of Dee.

[Note! A day after including this poem, I see an internet item on the history in Sweden of having women call the herds home with their vocalizations called KULNING. A domestic Scandinavian music form to call herds home and scare away predators. High pitched haunting tones to propagate sound over long distances. Kingsley's England had the River Dee which flowed to an estuary that became the border between Wales and England. This poem written in 1849 shows that Kulning made it to England.]

This poem's kulning is symbolic of so much in this GOMOL: gracenote-belongsong It carries within it the Tsunamic vision of a mix of climate, political, and contagion catastrophe that is brewing on this earth. Gaia is in pain. As I write, the news tells of over a million have died from coronavirus – and the coming winter season does not augur well. Yes, HUMAN DEATH is being capitalized with global interconnections. Our CALLING, as with a poem, is to get the "center to hold." Creating sounds to carry long distances.

When I discuss "poetries," I always have in mind a structure that holds and rings true to its "calling" and its own "call." This recalls – Addressor-Addressee-Addressoion as mentioned with Apollo. Indeed, every life has its own special "calling" and response to that calling. . .which issues its own call as the Addressoion which center-holds-expresses one's own life. Like Mary – we are subject to physical circumstance --- howsoever it manifests its consequences to us. That Syntangoion centering candle in the wind is vulnerable and lives with death's inevitability. Mary's gone, but she still calls the cattle home across the sands of time and in our consciousness. The "Holy Grail" of human life is the ability to advance living's Gracings over the Graves of our dying: to serve life in spite of death's final serve. I've called it our GEN-i-US as a species. --- Some people because of their special abilities and renown add more to life's symphonic movement than many, as I, who are but gracenotes, howsoever absorbed. Dmitry Shostakovich (1906-1975) composed his 14th Symphony while he was dying. He called it his "impassioned protest against death," and his "landmark piece." This – from Mark Wigglesworth's internet accounting adds its notes to GOTMOL:

"At the premiere, Shostakovich overcame his usual shyness to explain to the audience that 'life is man's dearest possession. It is given to him only once and he should live so as not to experience acute pain at the thought of the years wasted aimlessly or feel searing shame for his petty and inglorious past, but be able to say, at the moment of death, hat he has given all his life and energies to the noblest cause in the world – to fight for the liberation of humanity. I want listeners to this symphony to realize that 'life' is truly beautiful. My symphony is an impassioned protest against death, a reminder to the living that they should live honestly, conscientiously, nobly, never committing to a base act. This is very important for much time will pass before scientists have succeeded in insuring immortality. Death is in store of all of us and I for one do not see any good in the end of our lives. Death is terrifying. There is nothing beyond it.' – Shostakovich was arguing against the view that is some glorious beginning to the afterlife. He disagreed with all the composers who had portrayed death with music that was beautiful, radiant, and ecstatic. For him, death really was the end and he took that as an inspiration to make sure that he lived his to its full."

Behold! This image of Kulning! Hear the voice calling. I quoted the poem fully of Mary calling the cattle home, because it rings true to our ever-as-Orpheus "calling" across the sands of time for the best in our humanness to come home and to hold Protean Firm from our labors and loves. Musically in the musical HAIR, this sentiment is sung well:

> *Harmony and understanding*
> *Sympathy and trust abounding*
> *No more falsehoods or derisions*
> *Golden living dreams of visions*
> *Mystic crystal revelation*
> *And the mind's true liberation*
> *Aquarius, Aquarius. . . .*

While I'm quoting others, I will add at this point some of Herbert Read's conclusion to his book THE MEANING OF ART:

"No one can deny the profound inter-relation of artist and community. The artist depends on the community --- takes his tone, his tempo, his intensity from the society of which he is a member. But the individual character of the artist's work depends on more than these: it depends on a definite will-to-form which is a reflection of the artist's personality, and there is no significant art without this creative will. . . .The ultimate values of art transcend the individual and his time and circumstance. They express an ideal proportion or harmony which the artist can grasp only in virtue of his intuitive powers. . . .He accepts any conditions so long as they express his will-to-form. . . .It is his faith that those values are nevertheless among the eternal attributes of humanity." (p. 262)

The "eternal attributes of humanity," I have termed the SHOALS of WONTSUNODI -The Shinning Holds of Angelic Legacies of Wonders That Should Not Die & Of Things Coming Into Themselves By Belonging Together—OTCITBYBELTER. "Angelic" is tuned to "intuitive" and "muses" and sensations/gracings of "being held in the hold." Grace at table! Words of thanks! Holds of thankful hands around the table. Call it the SHOWONOTBYTANGO of The Only Known Home of Life in the Universe A spontaneous happening of everyday's crafting for the best. [Recall the story of Newlight's planning and crafting. The SYNTANGOION is there.]

!!!O! SHOWONOTBYTANGO of TOKHOLITU!!!

Our Time! Our Song! Our behold of some many wonders in precarious circumstances unknown to our humanity's past. With the tick-tocks of the Doomsday Clock getting louder, the fires and storms getting more destructive – and a plethora of climate-contagion issues and crises ever ascending – we are on notice to be agents of survival or not. Some say if we don't turn things around by 2050 we may have lost control of our climate and life-sustaining resources. The religions and fantasies penned thousands of years ago were of a different world – wherein, for most, a divine creator was in control of their promise and gave-out his punishment when they didn't perform. Such was their interpretation. The one thing they had a sense of and made much of was COVENANT – as basically a working relationship to prosper and stay out of trouble. Alas, that still pertains, but in a much different context of relationship, namely Humanity and Planet Earth. There is no greater challenge today than this: getting peoples globally to work out of today's context and its sciences, rather than that "other worldly" context so deep into the past. In many ways, I have reinstituted the concept of "covenant," because it is the ever-necessary action/concept for the "center to hold." That center is Humanity's TOKHOLITU. Hold-On! Hold-Tight!

Wake Up! Wake Up! The over-riding absolute law of existence is that life implies death. To live is to die. Stars-Galaxies-Peonies-Grizzlies-People!!!! The parallel law is that all this happens within the interplay of the random and the holistic -- until the release. A special law of consciousness applies where life (ants-birds-rodents) knows of the danger to it --- but more specially to that life, for such as we, that knows it will eventually die and attempts to live as gloriously as possible nonetheless. Humanity lives by an additional law: living for its own sake within death – but with a sense of making/living a life that transcends death and that has the intuitive fire of an eternity. The Dawn's on the Lawn.

The Opera Operative in every instance of these thoughts/laws is THE HOLD. There would be nothing if the stuff of existence didn't hold together by enchantments "of things coming into themselves by belonging together." (OTCITBYBELTER) By means of this ACE life's glories emerge. Thus and therefore – our special ACE of Now -- GOTMOL within THE HOLD. --- Ahhhh! To Have and to Hold. Till Death do Us Part. Ahhh! To love this life and the ever-going forward singing/marching to one's belongsong with its choral tones of lived integrity sounding in the Choir of Humanity for as long as it performs. -- O! To intone one's own sounding and thrust it into the abyss melodically-meaningfully-screamingly: one's gracenote held fast and true as added resonance within this symphony's composition played by these howsoevers to whatsoever end.

Withal, our song ever-calling the cattle home. Withal, the gracing "wind" beneath our wings. Every THRESHOLD a HOPE – Held by Our Passage's Embrace. "Ride, Baby, Ride!! That distance in you is never too far." Memory's chorus calls our horses home. Our courser prancing like a poem across the tides where eagles capture the wind.

I'm re-feeling my own faith in myself;
To trust without saddle, reins, or trusted spurs.
My arms fluttering like wings in the jumps
On a stallion's grace against the tides . . . .
[A Gracenote Holding On!]

(-- From the Soul's comments, above.)

This image is from the Disney film The Black Stallion: boy's arms waving in the air as they gallop-ride together after each found a trust that held them both – as the two freedoms felt the HELD of the HOLD. (Later, the boy named the stallion "The Black": You can watch it on the site for the movie.) Also, the art portrait created by Tom Chambers' Marwari Stallion is a beautiful take of the same theme with a young girl, arms extended like wings, on the black stallion riding gently with an eagle in the air. (This you can see on the artsy.net site and gilmancontemporary.com.) All such images – showing full trust in the relationship -- recall Martin Buber's concept of I-THOU from the HELD IN-THE-HOLD epiphanic moment with a horse.

When I wrote the above, some years ago, the Disney scene may have been in my memory. Prior to it were the classic Greek images on the immortal-winged-horses – ARION & PEGASUS. In my writings, I have emphasized ARION because that was also the name of an ancient Greek Poet. I've fused them with the name AROION – to reflect the SYNTANGOION in that concept.) What's the concept? The fusion of the human and natural world and our ever-continuing relationship that holds us as creatures on the same ride. Call it the domestication of wildness – in ourselves and earth's kingdoms of creatures and our shared environs: the ever-omnipresent fact of our shared Galactic-Gaia-Gallop. Our Destiny of Sharing -- with a trust-truth-tenacity that holds for the good of all. What's the concept? – IT'S the Hold & Freedom and the Physical & Consciousness – duets. The image above depicts the existential sync of THE HOLD & FREEDOM. As always, in such thought, the reciprocity of Immanence & Transcendence forges a particular, as yet incomprehensible but livable, Sentience. I call it IT'S. That "apostrophe" symbolizing our possessive & contracted -- Gracenote as an 'Apo'kstrophes'. We are still learning to ride a stallion that may always be as black as beautiful – bouncing as bountiful! HALLEHOLDON!

THE GRACENOTE CONTINUUM . . . .

O! I was writing/living/singing in the gracenote continuum long before I ever had this phrase to tone my belongsong. I use it to conclude GOTMOL as truly an-on-going phenomenon for all who have come to live in this theatrum mundi of the mysterium tremendum kosmosoion. It's one fantastic production and all who live get to add their belongsong's unique notation to the never-ending symphony of existence. Those listening to the wind with the feel of its bluster, will know that the sciences/technologies are taking-over from the scriptures of religions and outlandish mysticisms. Not to say that many will still believe traditionally. BUT! The daily "Holding" operation of planet-peoples is based, fundamentally, on the sciences and our technologies. Our daily GOTMOL is still vibrantly exercised by The Gracenote Continuum and all the arts and poetries still singing of the day's blessings and the candles for the dark vastness of the unknowns. – I repeat again, this excerpt from CONCORDIA HARMONIA DISCORS in *Sympathies* (p. 151):

> If there's nothing to know from where we stand,
> then there's nothing at all to understand.
> Each age is on call to make its best call
> and gather the fruits that shouldn't fall.
> Earth still spins lonely in deepest space
> no matter in what galaxies we show our face.
> New chemistries don't always mix
> with old formulas tradition fixed.
> New physics, meta and quantum, abound,
> but we still build homes right on the ground.
> Of possible places Earth's second to none,
> keeps spinning its spun, no place else to run.
> If there's something to know from where we stand,
> then there's something for all to understand.
> Since Earth's the only place we can call home
> we should live the grace, not tie-up the phone.
> If there's nothing to know frow where we stand
> then there's nothing at all to understand.
> Nothing at all, if on our magic planet's ride,
> we cast our hopes to the moon's other side.
> But we do know something from where we stand –
> there's no other place known where life's the plan:
> where truth and beauty have formed such a clan
> living past death and what we don't understand.
> > *"When They've All Had Their Quarrels And Parted*
> > *We'll Be The Same As We Started.*
> > *Just Travlin' Along, Singing A Song,*
> > > *Side By Side.*

Continuing with the GRACENOTE CONTINUUM and bringing that special something to the HOLD that truly holds ever so purely and gently. Alas, I find at this juncture that this Celtic Blessing sings a true belongsong.

May the strength of the wind and
the light of the sun,
The softness of the rain and
the mystery of the moon
Reach and fill you.
May beauty delight you and
happiness uplift you,
May wonder fulfill you and
love surround you.
May your step be steady and
your arm be strong.
May your heart be peaceful and
your word be true.
May you seek to learn,
may you learn to live,
May you live to love, and
may you love ~~ always.

It carries no theology or difficult comprehension. It is as natural as sunlight and the laughter of children and every variety of cuddling and caressing one can imagine. It's easy to feel here the clarity of mind and the music of breathing as these gracenotes play into the larger symphony. Here's my recent GOTMOL from MOM:

IF I SHOULD LIVE ANOTHER DAY

If I should live another day.
It will be to love another day:
Some tomorrow in the present.
Some potent beyond yesterday.

If I should live another day,
Rise with the dawn, breathe the dare,
It will be to love another day
Beholden by the hold of care.

For sure I'd live for another day
Another chance to rhyme my say,
Here the music of timeless romance –
Holding life in my arms for one more dance.

If I should live another day,
I'll give no thought of going away –
Just grasp again the promise to cope;
By light of day – the caress of hope.

IF I SHOULD LIVE TO LOVE ANOTHER DAY

This is the Burney Relief – a Mesopotamian terracotta relief – of around 1800-1750 BCE. Go to the internet for a full story. It's here just to emphasize the "holding" it represents while keeping the beasts controlled and the owls in control as she, Ishtar (Lilith, Inanna, Ereshkigal ???), is Goddess of the Night – perhaps returning from the nether world. A worship piece for sure. Three rings on each writ and three taloned bird feet as the owls. She's holding measuring tools, used in building, by one theory. Probably Minoan Master of the Animals (1700-1500BCE) here as well. A good example of "re- lig-ion": re-tying, re-binding: THE HOLD on display. Also, all such artistic manifestations of the female and her power include the implicit womb-hold-release of progeny. A very magical thing to frame in the context of the othernesses of existence. Such an angel visited Mother Mary, perhaps.

ATHENA -- Another feminine display of THE HOLD, but with different, but connected, approach is the Greek's ATHENA --- The Goddess of War and Wisdom. So, the wondering, what's the connect of war and wisdom and her OWL, which symbolizes/actualizes this relationship. Here's Athena as often depicted. Take a look. My photo of her in my study. My explanation below.

The Owl is known for not only looking wise – with eyes wide open – but it's a well endowed bird of prey (terrific hearing, seeing, sensing) that works the darkness (as does the Firefly, and our theories of existence). Athena is equipped for war (defense of wisdom, prosperity, and futures). They both come from a world based on predation for survival. Humanity and the natural world are thus related and orchestrated. Her eyes and those of the owl are focused on the wisdom-wars of survival and prosperity. You can see THE HOLD. They are in the hold of struggle and victory. When I say of the POET – Passage Owl of Epiphanic Tang – I have the caress of these two in mind. In this era of COVID-19, this intense combined-covenantal focused-HOLD is required. Indeed, in this pandemic era wisdom is at war with planetary contagions. Now, another chapter.

A MINI-ESSAY-SONG OF THE "HALLE" JUBILANT GOTMOL
A SAID-SUNG HALLELUJAH HOWSOEVER IT RINGS ONE'S BELLS
WITH MEMORIES OF HOPES AND HOLDINGS OF HANDS ACROSS THE SANDS

I N T R O

Whatever the composition of existence,
The secret of our persistence
Snow to rain, joy to sorrow,
Sunshine days with promises of tomorrows --
We are the choir the voices the composers
We – the Mortals of the Music,
The Poets of Portals and Portends
We the instruments forming the bells,
Ringing the bells – being inspired by the bells --
Clanging strophes beyond catastrophes!

T O A N D F R O

We are the Jubliants of Hallelujahs
Joyfully lifting our arms in praise and celebration
Even with destinies of death and destruction
And a universe of darknesses in every direction
Singing, now –right here, in GOTMOL --
The 301st version of the Hallelujah Chorus,
From Cohen through the SHERK to today's
Lu Lu Ooo Ooo duet of Legend and Underwood.
We're a pandemic of groans and glorias
Singing through our 2020 masks today.
There's a virus vexing our voices today
A hoping for shots to keep death at bay
But we're holding-on and standing tall
Withal and the 300 versions
Of Hallelujah choruses! Go listen to some!
HALLE HALLE HALLE LU L U LU JAH JAH JAH
The planet is a farm we are the farmers
The planet is a family and we its progeny
The planet is a climate and we its mate
Of such our voices should grow louder
Singing Our Song of Earth and Us – Us and Earth . . . galloping prouder!

O U T R O

We're holding tight and together – Ride baby Ride!
Singing afresh the Hallelujah Chorus – That Distance in you is never too far!

HalleholdYou –

HalleHoldMe

HalleholdUs –

HalleholdWe

HALLEHOLDON!

HALLEHOLDON ! HALLE – H OOO O L D – ON ! – HALLEHOLDON !

HOLD THAT NOTE!

45

GLOSSARY

PRELUDE

Fondly they asked the truth of truth's deep truth;
Were rigorously told that which is true
Has undeconstructable memoried truth,
Such that truth unfudged is truth unbudged –
Baritoned by your own soprano I:
Homoousious Homoiosious:
Animus & Umbilicus Mundi;
Our Happy Meals pattied between the buns,
Pickled with Plato's truth that it's not the words,
But what they sing along with the howling of the wind –
As by any "I" twixt any "O's."

CODA

Witnesses found it had to determine,
Having left their dictionaries at home,
What they had really drunk from truth's deep well;
If they'd just wetted their whistles once more
For another bold jingle in the dark,
Or were re-baptized with re-christened words
Thant grinned Mona-sinless from their canvassed
Disegnols – still easeled, but not hung-up –
Showing the brush-marks of fresh passages
On multi-undercoats of truth's bravura.
Still, they bravoed "Encore! Rare Done!" Then they
Offered prayers to transcend catachresis.

[From – 'Oh, Well!!(Sung with deepest Homages and Apologies to all." –*Altarpieces*, p.188/190.) A reminder that my word-phrase creations are to enhance comprehension and imagination – with no expectations of inclusion in tomorrow's dictionaries.]

Acronyms&Amalgams&Neologisms are as sprinkles of stardust-sunshine-hearthtones – better known as "gracenotes," or "fairies," "daimoions," or "angelic fluterances." Additives like a shake of cinnamon and a touch of brandy to enhance your wassail: savings of left-overs to fertilize your garden – aroma your soups. Alas, to wake-up what embeds in efficacy and the ineffable. Let it shine its time. Glistenings to reveal the rime.

ANSWER – A New Spirituality We Are

ACE – Astonishing Covenantal Embrace – Rhymes with Amazing Continuum's Grace

AFIRADAPO – A Fireflies At Dawn Poiesis This is the Domaine/Domain Name, as it were, for all my books.

ALPHA – [a] – name-letter designation og the Fundamental-Fine-Structure-Constant

'APO'KSTROPHES' – Universal (ALPHA)Name for Poets of the Poioema

ADDRESSOION – That Middle Candle Flame from the interplay of Addressor and Addressee

AXOIONS – Theoretical particles causing the holds to become mass

AROION—The Ancient Poet (Arion)& Ancient Horse (Arion) of Immortality

AWEAEWA – Augural Wisdom Energies – Palindrome/Pendulum

ANEMOION – The Four Winds

Acheiropoieton – Not Made by Human Hands – The HOLD is such. We sure use it.

APE – AutoPoeticEssay – Poem as essay with Autobiographical touch

BELONGSONG – Sung/Felt/Lived – It is the (soul) harmony of Belonging

BOD – Bard Ovate Druid (The "bod" as resident in TOE-GUT-HEAD)

BOHOCO – BOnd-HOld-COvenanat

COVNAT – Covenant with Nature

COHO – COvenantal HOld –COHOCO --COnsciousness

COVENATOION – act of Covenanting as with OiO

COVE – Covenant/Covenance – Covenend (other than Reverend -- Cove vs. Rev.) Reverence as Covenance

COVID – Covenantally Inspired Destiny

EPITOFITME – Any entity as its Epitome being the fittest hold for survival, eg. – a cardinal's redness, a rhino's horn -- a human's consciousness

EMINENCE – one's victorious-balanced-focused hold midst complexity, promise and the inevitable. Alas, an accomplished EPITOFITME of any species and individual of such is an achieved EMINENCE.

DAWN'S BALM ON THE LAWN – Shining primal reality of life on earth—Immanence! As SONG – pronounced SO-DA-BA-O-LA!

FIFORONAT – Any Fifth Force of Nature as conceived … Quintessentially

GRACE – Keystone word/concept of the ACE – Astonishing Covenantal Embrace -- Call it the Grand Romance of ACE – A caressing Aura of holding gratitude

GRACINGS – Any variety of tones and groceries that gracenote our belongsong

GOTMOL – Gracing Our Time's Meaning Of Life

GRACENOTE –unique belongsong flourish that graces the larger symphony of life

GEN-i-US – The new Generation designation for all ages in this present era and its need for a Humanity of Genius to solve life's newest challenges for a promising future

GOD – The traditional concept "beheld" of a HOLDER beyond The Hold, because we so keenly experience by our being held -- the persistence to be so verses not to be so. The Unknown Holding

Pattern's Ultimate Will To Form – that's beyond THE HOLD we experience; and beyond the god-goddess-divine law presence many interpret from this Hold. But that Ultimate Will (as Intentional) is beyond our knowing or concrete experience. Belief can do it! Poetries can sing in and around it. Science hasn't seen it. Intellect can't comprehend it. GOD—Groceries On Demand-Gracings Of Destiny. Glistening Of Dawn

GREUKS – Greening Eurekas

GREGRAGRO – Greening-Gracing-Groceries

HEAD - Holoistoions Evolutionary Aligned Destiny – realities evolving to holistic alignments that make them what they are

HOLISTOIONS – Active holistic-holding of life – The OiO interplay of sunshine, atmosphere, gardening mind and mud for the harvest than nourishes

HOLOMOVEMENT – The Bohm concept based on his concept of Implicate Order, which is in all due respects is the same and THE HOLD.

HARP – *harmonia praestebilia*

HEAD-HA-HO – HEAD as defined above with the holding pattern of harmonic tonalities—HARP-HOLD

HOLOCOHO – Holistic Covenantal Hold

HUG2BE – Humanity's Ultimate Grace To Belong (therefore 2B)

HUGS OF COHOCO AT HOME IN TOKHOLITU - Humanity's Universal Global Summons of Covenantal Holding Consciousness at Humanity's Own Mother Earth in The Only Known Home Of Life In The Universe

HIDDEN-DOWN – from the "poetry" meaning all the HA-HO within the human body as a mirroring-like function of all beyond this "hidden down"

HAPE-HOME – Home Address Planet Earth--Humanity's Own Mother Earth

THE HOLD – Call it Holdings Of Life's Designs – the everywhere/everyday force in existence that hold things together – even if only to release realities consistently to death -- but, even so, The Hold persists to Hold for new life to form – as Humanity's Own Living Destiny – Alas, a phrase that holds its own as THE HOLD.

HALLEHOLDYOU – HALLEHOLDUS – HALLEHOLDME - HALLEHOLDWE ---

HALLEHOLDON -- Hallelujah Chorus for The Hold (Hold those notes!)

HOPE – Humanity's Own Promising Embrace

HOLD THE FOLD -- graces gathered and herded in collective embrace

INTERSTITIUM – theorized organ that holds/feeds all body organs

ION -- suffix of action happening now

IMMANENCE – The Hold is within all existences. Our self-objective-consciousness of it seems the threshold of being HELD leading to feelings/thoughts of transcendence.

KULNING – the strident melodic voice projections to call the herds and cattle home

LIDADIL/DILALID – this LifeInDeath/DeathInLife, etc. is the reciprocal dynamic that is visualized as a pendulum swinging to-and-fro in this palindromic holding pattern – the "A" is that pivotal phenomenon of "auguries" and the 'Apo'strophes' grasp of the meaning: it is also the manifest "i" in the OiO reciprocillations

MOIORA – name for the winds at one's back and in one's face

MOIOKE – rhymes with Karaoke – interactive singing/singer in pub or bar.

MOM ZIE KAI -- From *Perhaps It's Just A Whim Poem?* In POP and AUGURIES. Briefly: Time-Spirit-Rose – Le Moment-Zietgeist-Kairos. My favorite exclamation to acknowledge the truth-tones of time's "eternal now" as it's happening.

MDOK – Manifest Destiny's Odyssean Kairos

OTCITBYBELTER – Of Things Coming Into Themselves By Belonging Together

OIO – If I could, I'd put these, here, in the form of the Syntangoion, which they – from ancient Greek's 9th letter that became the "iota" twist the "O's" of the Council of Nicea's "homoIousius: Father and Son not the same, but in the hold of "likeness." The Church didn't go with Arian's "likeness – iota." But I've carried forth the OIO as designation of the Syntangoion's play in concepts. Somewhat like a Robin with both a worm and a seed in its beak. Or just a flaming I AM twixt polarities.

PROCOHO – Protect-Comprehend-Hold On-To

POIOEMA -- Domain of Crafted Poetry

POIOESIS – Creation of poetries as in POET

PENTAMAROION – Detailed in AUGURIES see note below this Glossary

POANSWER –Poetries Of A New Spirituality

POEM – Peace On Earth Music

POEMS – Passages Of Epochal Menses

POET – Passages Owl of Epiphanic Tang

POETIC JUSTICE – Rhymes of structures and their senses providing directives of existential integrity

QUINTETOION -- This is the Breathing/Meditative sequence/structure that I use throughout each day – ever since finding/first conceptualizing it in ALTARPIECES -2011. It is one of my most fundamental grasps of THE HOLD and the inhalation-exhalation reciprocillation of the universe. Five instruments with seven sounds: (1-in)AH-HA!(Two sounds of Inspiration/Aspiration)—(2-out)CHI (Oriental sound of Energy/Forces) –(3 in0) A-U-M(the three Vedic primal sounds of existence) – (4 out)JAAAHHH (divinity "AH" sound found in most relgions/spiritualizations): (5 throughout) fifth instrument is THE HOLD as the holistic dynamics over the whole and between each of the instruments. I breathe so as daily discipline doing whatever. . . including prior to sleep. When used specific to meditation, I put each thumb between each hand's four fingers, which symbolized the physicality of the hold and the five instruments. This done – the hands can be placed howsoever to feel that ACE!

REHEDE – Real Heal Deal

RESBYDES – Resilience By Design

RERERE – THREE "Rs" –Reason-Renaissance-Resilience – Reason, often, as Reverence

RECIPROCILLATION – the constant back and forth give and take to take and give. Term is to give more truth to the interchange dynamic than mere oscillation or mutual interchange. Reciprocity, as such, is a "holding dynamic" that holds "holistically" -- as it's own reality -- over and through the interplay of polarities.

RELEASE – This relates to death as the hold releasing is hold. It also relates to various psychological conditions – bi-polar-suicidal-depression --- whereby the individual has lost stable mooring is and is adrift. This term arises naturally and the polar opposite to the hold. It is a new term, somewhat, and will have more exploration in the future – by both the sciences and the poetries. If anything, it helps comprehend the hold. This GOTMOL does but wave recognition of this realm of thought.

SYNTANGOION – the synergistic tangooion dance of opposites to manifest the standing "I" that give them and the relationship meaning. Takes two to dance as one.

SHOALS OF WONTSUNODI – Shining Holds of Angelic Legacies of Wonders That Should Not Die.

SOUL – Consciousness and Creatureliness in feels-held Harmonious Focus: one's Being radiant with time's eternal now. See transcendence below. Song Of Universal Longing/

SHOWONCITER – Shoals of Angelic Legacies of Wonders That Should Not Die & Of Things Coming Into Themselves By Belonging Together

STRUCTURE – The manifests the HOLD in everything…and everything has formed to the form it is because of the HOLD. Truth-Beauty-Justice – like flowers-birds-Fords – are structures with holding patterns. – Poetry/Music/Art are crafts committed to structuring in language/sound/sight that which manifests from the HOLD and needs a capture of the luster that holds it like a hold of Proteus which causes him to prophesy.

SEVENTH SENSE – As described – this is THE HOLD that holds all the other five and the IAM as one.

SUPERNATURAL – highest orders of Human&Nature working reciprocally: the absolute superlative best concert of being/performing naturally -- here and now.

TOKHOLITU – This Only Know Home Of Life In This Universe

TANGO – TAO – In the Flow it takes two "holding-on"to dance its will to form.

TRANSCENDENCE – That Held in place lifted feeling when one holds all the aces and rises above circumstance. Meditation does this. An Ah-Ha moment does this.feeling of accomplishment and being truly at Home – does this. The Held and the Soul are one.

A special group of terms relating to THE HOLD and a UNIFIED THEORY HOLOCENE-ANTHROPOCENE-BIOGENESIS-BIOPOIESIS-NOOSPHERE-BIOSPHEREIC-FINE STRUCTURE TUNING-QUANTUM HOLOGRAPHY -- Ecosphere/biosphere/lithosphere/geosphere/hydrosphere/atmosphere/heliosphere

"Gray is the dogma, but green is the Tree of Life." Goethe

Walt Whitman, in the 1860's, did speak of such a take and so said he: "We must have new words, new potentialities of speech . . . The new times, the new people need a new tongue according, and what is more, they will have such a tongue --- will not be satisfied until it is evolved." -- Our Time is such a New Time! We need another Whitman-Emerson duet.

NOTES FOR THE JOURNEY OF MANIFEST DESTINY'S ODYSSEAN KAIROS

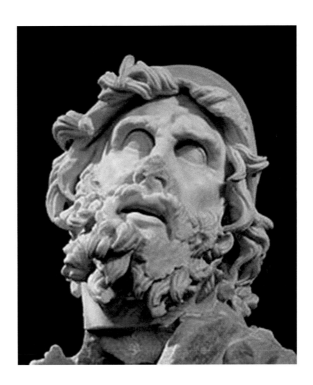

ODYSSEUS

Seems the concept of THE HOLD got its formation in Auguries in this way: from the interplay of PREDATION & PROCREATION there arose the PROPEROION(1) prosperity/hope/promise – from which emerged the SHOWONAKARION (2), which was a trinity hold of SHOALS -WONTSUNDI & AROCKAKORA (Augural Recrecendoes of Covenantal Kairos). These four were then held as one, encased/enfolded/enchoired, by a fifth dimension termed the PENTAMAROION (3), which is the "holding" Breath-Breathing quintessence of life – inhalation-exhalation. – From this formed the trinity of these three developments (AS NUMBERED) from the predation-procreation dance: as the PROSHOPENTION. All together: THE HOLD. –MDOK—Here are some notes.

Note: Mihaly Csikszentmihakyi is well-known for his writing on the concept of FLOW, which is primarily a psychological concept of giving-in to the self-creative process where challenge and response are in common focus, clarity, balance, and a sense of being truly at home with oneself. I emphasize Getting Hold Of One's Self as primary. We know by the holding of another's hands if that hold is right for continuance. The evolutionary process of creative growth is indeed best with such a flowing sensation that knows it's on the right track. This Flow, however conceived, issues forth from those holdings in place that constitute the field where the growing takes place and can take hold. --- Mihaly and I are of the same age. I would love to dialogue/debate with him how the Hold is primary to the Flow – and in fact makes the Flow possible. We are both discussing/comprehending the process by which things/thoughts/etc. come into themselves by belonging together. Some things balance and some don't. If the balance holds then the "thresholds of flow" can continue. If there are holding patterns that HOLD – then life can proceed. Sperm and Ova have to form the Child-Hold before the Child can sense the flow. Alas, from the womb-hold thrown into a life to find what holds still. In brief, I sense the Flow is basically getting Hold of one's self in the midst of complexities and therefore to be at Home while finding one's own pathway to the future. Having a hand-railing as one is walking-up the stairs is good --- very good. A good foothold on life's shifting stones is good. Psychological counseling begins with what holds and structures one's life so that one feels held. Knowing the dollar's value – one can better spend it well. –Songs of Dawn's Balm On The Lawn!

Note: Newton's third law: for every action there's an equal and opposite reaction. – This in embodied in my Syntangoion. Existence seems to embody this law as it pits polarity against polarity: some verses none. The only answer to why it is so is that it is so to be so. Understandings of this "holding pattern" is our living's journey incarnate and ever-ascending. It's great to have a home even though we are always cleaning house.

Note: From Wikipedia this terse summation: "….time cannot be separated from 3-D because the observed rate at which time passes for an object depends on the object's velocity relative to the observer. --- General relativity also provides an explanation of how gravitational fields can slow the passage of time for an object as seen by an observer outside the field." – Therefore, "spacetime is a manifold of four dimensions." --- Alas, "focused" observers measuring the observed are manifests of time itself, which – howsoever in passage – is also the sea that holds our ship with destinations in the hold.

Note: My website article THE EMBRACE OF THE HOLD has much more on this subject as it relates to the Fifth Force of Nature. – The FIFORONAT. Here's a note from there.

Seems scientists working with Helium released a boson (not a dark photon messenger as from other findings) some 33 times heavier and more energetic than an electron. They called it X17---a protophobic X boson. In quantum physics. "bosons are particles. . .that carry energy and function as the 'glue' that 'holds' matter together and controls the interactions between physical forces." (From BigThink-1/11/19) Seems there is a "hidden layer" called the "dark sector" of the quantum world that doesn't interact in some normal way with our observable, standard model universe. Scientist J. L. Feng (SciNews, 8/10/16) said "it's possible that these two sectors talk to each other and interact with one another through somewhat veiled but fundamental interaction." Readers will easily see how these statements refer to THE HOLD as that force that has to be there. Such would be a fifth Force of Nature - that Quintessence-Omnipresence is always searched for and theorized. If truly found it would unify all the forces of nature and radically transform our concept of existence. Seems the forces of nature, except gravity, are powered by bosons –THE GLUE THAT HOLDS MATTER TOGETHER AND CONTROLS THE INTERACTIONS.

Here, in GOTMOL as in the EMBRACE essay, I've seen due cause to say poetically/philosophically, with the help of science, that THE HOLD, more than metaphorically, characterizes/conceives that 5th Force: from the ancient quintessence to today's most recent findings. Of course, this new boson emanation from Helium awaits more confirmation – if at all. Even so, it joins the on-going reality finds that indicate "some" 5th Force that's holding reality together – galaxies to giraffes, peonies to people. How this 5th force works with the 7th sense and holistic tertium quid of all interactions – is for the scientists of elegant mathematics to formulate. They are perhaps but as metaphoric measures of the hiddenness in THE HOLD, which, elegantly, unhides for us every day in every which way. – And don't forget that "tertium quid" prevailing "something" that always remains when the polarities "something & nothing" do their annihilations. Every event is ultimately a "something." Seems "something" will always "hold on." Oh! Opus Tripartium Totus Tuus! Now, to talk of the 11th Hour – is to have Embraced all five primes 3-5-7-9-11. – The ultimate significance of this is yet to be grasped.

MY BOOKS

GLISTENINGS 2010 – My wife Marilyn's Requiem
ALTARPIECES 2011 – First of OPUS TRIPARTIUM TOTUS TUUS
SYMPATHIES 2014 – Second of OPUS TRIPARTIUM TOTUS TUUS
AUGURIES 2017 – Third of OPUS TRIPARTIUM TOTUS TUUS
MOM 2020 – First Collection – Muse of Mortality 6/19
POP 2020 – Second Collection – Poetries On Purpose 8/29
SOS 2020 – Third Collection – Song Of Songs 10/10
GOTMOL 2020 – Somewhat of a summation of all the above. 12/1
More on my website – mdokelly.com

A concluding note at this "MY" time and this time in America and World history. I'm 86 now and counting each day. I think everything I've written and will still write if I have more time – is a love song trying to be more beautiful and more just: A BETTER HOLD. A Better Dancing Partner. Presently, I've no readers of my works except a few friends and some family: and they partially. I don't know of any others and don't expect to have any. One needs connections and marketing capabilities I don't possess. Well, I don't write for the crowd. I plan to wave my flag a bit when/if possible. I would really like a dialogue about my concepts and presentation. Criticism! Refinement! I don't write to make money and will never come close to collecting what I've paid to publish. I got into the self-publishing business thinking I'd like to see my writing published while I'm still around. Well, surprise Me! I'm still around! And still no sales of any book that I know of. Now, GOTMOL gets closer to being ready to print and to begin the New Year. I'm its only Editor and sure to miss a syntax-typo. Meaning prevails!

Now, to OUR TIME. There are denials of science, various violences and conspiracies that legitimate violence. There are climate and global accord challenges with opposing sides. And there is the coronavirus contagion in the mix with political contagions. Yesterday's normal seems some distance in the future – if ever to return. Seems unlikely – all things considered. There is a spiritual-religious problem on this planet as more and more find less and less to justify some distant Divinity playing puppeteer with peoples lives: some to die too soon horribly or howsoever as others live and thrive. Criticism of religious dogma stirs religious violence in some. Current events between the French and Muslim terrorists and the expansion of "hate" groups in America come from this. Furthermore, our advanced telescopes and technologies solve nothing of those dynamics. They say we are alone and on our own on this lonely planet like a speck of dust in a random whirlwind. There's a traffic-jam at the crossroads of an unprecedented era in human affairs and livelihood. Horns are blaring-out for a truer meaning of life and its program.

In the meantime the Tsunami is rising and we must take hold of our awareness and stratagems for survival of Life On Earth. Japan is housing some 17,000 tons of nuclear waste that will have to go somewhere other than the ocean where it will cause major destructive "hold" problems. The Hold, recall, is in every action in existence – some are dangerous to planet and humanity, while at the same time being the power behind/within all that is good and that "graces" our meaning of life. The coronavirus is bad and the vaccines against it are good: both embody THE HOLD function to be what they can be. The State of Michigan has banned the possession of the Marble Crayfish due to its propagation and destructive capabilities to other wildlife. It is a parthenogenetic female that produces some 700 eggs each reproductive cycle – creating identical offspring that can easily become overwhelmingly destructive. So, another example of how The Hold works that is not generally beneficial -- challenging us for knowledge and control. Some is of our own making. Nicholas Carr, in his "GLASS GAGE: How Computers Are Changing Us," is saying we can break-out of being dominated by our advancing technologies: use then to enhance life's fulfillments and potentials for human prosperity and freedom – rather than becoming captive to AI and have our own control of our destiny mechanized. He writes, as follows:

"This tension between what the body can accomplish and what the mind can envision is what gave rise to and continues to propel and shape technology. It's the spur for humankind's extension of itself and elaboration of nature. Technology isn't what makes us 'posthuman' or 'transhuman,' as some writers and scholars have recently suggested. It's what makes us human. Technology is in our nature. Through our tools we give our dreams form. The practicality of technology may distinguish it from art, but both spring from a similar, distinctly human yearning." (p. 215) "Automation severs ends from means. It makes getting what we want easier, but it distances us from the work of knowing. . . .By reclaiming our tools as parts of ourselves, as instruments of experience rather than just means of production, we can enjoy the freedom that congenial technology provides when it opens the world more fully to us." (p.232) When Carr writes of "the work of knowing" and "congenial technology," he comes close to expressing THE HOLD & GOTMOL. Knowing is holding. Congenial is being held. Twenty-eight years before Carr, William Barrett wrestled with the same situation in his "DEATH OF THE SOUL: From Descartes to the Computer":

"The dreamers of the computer insist that we will someday be able to build a machine that can take over all the operations of the human mind, and so in effect replace the human person. . . . But in the course of these visions they forget the very plain fact of the human body and its presence in and through consciousness . . . . If . . .ever realized it would be a curiously disembodied kind of consciousness, for it would be without the sensitivity, intuitions, and pathos of our human flesh and blood. And without those qualities we are less than wise, certainly less than human." (p.160-161)

Indeed, the workings of such a holding pattern as THE SOUL – sensitivity-intuition-pathos-flesh-blood – is the human "work of knowing" that becomes THE HOLD &GOTMOL. Barrett gave this conclusion (p.160):

"Finally, to bring this tedious business to its conclusion, there is the fact of what may loosely be called the poet's development. The poet changes, ages, matures—and sometimes ripens into wisdom …. How much of our consciousness is embedded in and inseparable from this fleshly envelope that we are? Certainly it is not the poet's business to write as a disembodied spirit. He falls in love, suffers, and his body ages---sometimes into the ripeness of vision: 'Bodily decrepitude is wisdom,' wrote Yeats, who turned the afflictions of old age into great poetry. But a machine cannot age this way."

Nineteen years (1926) before Barrett, Arthur Koestler wrote "THE GHOST IN THE MACHINE" – the "ghost" being the destructive tendencies of opposites within the human world. Koestler did this work without even examining the "predatory" dimension of the creatures of existence – including humans. Also, his thought preceded the world of AI and machine-to-machine learning. However, he did make an approach to the concept of THE HOLD:

"But there is no satisfactory word in our vocabulary to refer to these Janus-faced entities(the 'masters' versus the 'servants' in hierarchically held structures – my summation): to talk of sub-whole (or sub-assemblies, sub-structures, sub-skills, sub-systems) is awkward and tedious. It seems preferable to coin a new term to designate these nodes . . . partially as wholes or wholly as parts…. The term I world propose is 'holon', from the Greek *holos* = whole, with the suffix *on* which, as in prot*on* or neutr*on*, suggest a particle or part. --- 'A man', wrote Ben Jonson, 'coins not a new word without some peril; for if it happens to be received, the praise is but moderate; if refused, the scorn is assured.' Yet I think the holon is worth the risk. . . .It also symbolizes the missing link . . . between the atomistic approach of the Behaviourist and the holist approach of the Gestalt psychologist. . . .both failed to take into account the hierarchic scaffolding of intermediate structures of sub-wholes." (p. 48-49) ---- [Ahhh! Many new words in my works and GOTMOL. I forgot some in my "Auguries" Glossary and perhaps some here as well. I hear – "Enough! Enough!"]

Wait! One more word, SUPERNATURAL, with some help from Aldous Huxley's *Literature And Science* (published the year he dies at age 69- 1963). GOTMOL is a book joining science and literature (physics/poetics) in the concept of THE HOLD – as both objective and private reality. He wrote: "The proper study of mankind is Man and, next to Man, mankind's properest study is Nature . . . of which he is an emergent part. . . must live in harmony. . . . Nature. . .is a system of dynamic balances, and, when a state of equilibrium has been disturbed, there is always attempts to establish a new balance between the forces involved. . . Between some classes of observed facts and some. . . of felt values, certain bridges ("Golden Mean") are discernable. For the literary artist. . . the existence of such bridges is a matter of highest importance." (p.110). THE HOLD is such a bridge. Being of highest importance – it is super - - - natural. Huxley is a good read for the beginnings of ecological thinking.

Surely, you can see the connections of these authors to the tale as I've tried to tell it of what holds us together. Koestler (he would go wild with all the supplement medications of today) proposed a medical solution for "the transformation of *homo maniacus* into *homo sapiens*." Some medication to quell the quakings of the mind and generate a transcendent holding (Golden Mean wholeness) – as if to concoct the alchemists dream of an *elixir vitae*. Huxley wrestled with such a Brave New World. The transcendence, of course, being earthly immanent as that flaming candle twixt the contrasting polarities of life represented in the SYNTANGOION. The challenge to humanity that these thinkers wrestled with is more than concretized as the COVID-19 pandemic has revolutionized our awareness to "Stand Tall! Hold Tight! midst Our Time's Tsunamic Warnings in our Eartharian ocean of science and spirituality. Candle-Torch-Lantern!! Let There Be Light!

THE LIGHTHOUSE TSUNAMI

https://www.boredpanda.com/lighthouse-photography/

BEHOLD! THE HOLD OF THE HELD HOLDING FOR THE HOLD OF THE BELONGSONG SINGING!

HALLEWEHOLDON!

POETIC JUSTICE

This is where 'Apo'kstrophes', ACE in the HOLD and SYNTANGOION come together—bringing all the other dimensions -- to harmonize as the epitofitme of BELONGSONG. The primal poet in the covenantal embrace of humanity's only living destiny – joins the dance of synergies to structure a flaming torch that enlightens the way through the dark into the light of day and a balanced chorus of that "silver lining" belongsong's belong-beholds. --- Of course, this all happens within the en-choirings and ALTAR gatherings of the temple, the shrine, cathedral – SANCTUARY – of one's SELF in a HOLDING-PATTERN (including the structured breathing of the QUINTETOION) with the world and others. There the songs-rhetorics-poetries-constructs-dreams are structured like songs-poems-symphonies-philosophies-laws!!! works of art as manifestations of the *holon* Will-to-Form as Belongsongs sung by a Choir! HALLEHOLDYOU!

This is poetic justice at work – because this is beauty, truth and belonging winning with a "holding" structure -- the likes of which is the source of Love itself. Like a poem, where the structure-sound-rhyme are in sync with the subject and its singing truth tones. Churches, religions, have the power they do because they are harmonically structured to hold people in place with an an ascending candle twixt life&death confrontations. Such scenes, scenarios, and inner-sanctums give life and truth to Poetic Justice in a world of unknowns, death, and random events. A well-crafted poem, as described, is a symbol of Poetic Justice…with its justifications of harmony, truth, beauty, and a humanity's belongsong for real. Such in our age of ecological-economical justice issues.

Alas, the upholding of what is most worthy is upheld. In spite of death, life continues victoriously. Poetic Justice is when the gracing of our time's meaning of life victoriously outclasses the deterrents and confusions. In the throws of such to find one's belongsong is Poetic Justice. This phrase has a lot of history and usage. Here, it exceeds the literary-judicial (even tennis) – to be a life-line of existential victory from quotidian to quantum to quintessence to IQ. -- In AUGURIES I composed a 7 page APOETESSAY(aka APE) entitled *The Point of No Return –A Sidebar WhackO In The Court of Poetic Justice.* Ahh! Climate Justice! Poetry & Science dancing and whacking "side-by-side." Here's an excerpt.

IT'S BREAK POINT, PJ!

Fault serves in an insane world just won't play.
This issue's always at break-point, PJ.
Clearly the old calling of Common Faith
Finds *unia sympathetica* with Common Ground,
Where our dead are loud as gods are mute.
Our lonely planet's getting lonelier,
As galaxies expand far past the far.
Earth Angels are hoarse from crying aloud!
Wings cramped by randoms of the mundane bad!
So much terror in our jurisprudence.
So much jurisprudence in our terror.
Surveillance spies on it own democracy!
MORE JUICE FOR *jus inter gentes* PJ!!!!!!
THE GLACIERS ARE MELTING . . . AWAY!
How now to rouse people so consumerized,
Super-natralized, super-jingoized,
Super-dogmatized, super-sexualized,
So virtual reality fantasized . . . .
WHEN ALL LIFE'S ON TRIAL?
What jury-choir is this writ preaching to PJ?
Who hasn't seen Earth through Apollo's eyes?
Old Blue Marble rolled in everyone's pocket,
Rumbling loud visions in everyone's socket
BEAUTY'S A DUTY AND TRUTH'S A CAREER!
BE THE MAGIC WAND – OR BOTH DISAPPEAR!
BIODIVERSITY IS LOSING ITS PLAY TODAY!
The World's Open's still Open and Hopin' –
Our serve connects on the ball that's droppin'!
Time for a service of aces, PJ.
Victory wants its glad past the daily sad.
Miserere! Miserere! Rhymes too much with Destiny! Destiny!
Gavel to the Anvil, PJ!
Time for a literature engage!
Time for a resistance spiriuelle!
You're the grantor of poetic license!
You're the *judicium totos tuus.*
Time to find your rhythm. Get a game plan.
WE ARE NOW AT THE(challenge&response)POINT OF NO RETURN.
LOVE! LOVE! LOVE! (*Respondeo, ergo sum!*) *IT'S BREAK POINT, PJ!*

GRAND CRU GRACE DU JOUR

This GOTMOL is nearly finished and it's now 12/1/20 in a world wrestling with the contagions of COVID-19, climate change, political upheavals, and changing concepts of life's meaning. All of these are impacted-illumined by the advances/revelations from the sciences. To mention gracing in our time is to take a renewed look at the meaning of life. Denials of realities are really inexcusable given the credible sources of information at our fingertip-internet. The same technology is available to those who fabricate, lie, and manipulate these concerns --- and is therefore added to the list of contagions operative in today's world. One must be careful on any slippery stone precipice.

The term "grand cru," which means "great growth" – can be applied to many creations other than wine – but most generally to a vineyard with a most favorable reputation in wine production. Daily, one maintains one's own "great growth." And that' a GOTMOL. But there's more. I'm bringing the concept/reality of vineyard in view because of the wild-gigafires of forests and vineyards in the West this summer of 2020. While some vineyards have been destroyed --- such fires, and hurricanes, tornadoes are becoming more frequent and more destructive worldwide. There is a terror in the "terroir" – the territory/landscape/vineyard where the grapes are grown.

Here's the connection. Virgil wrote GEORGICS from 38-32- BCE. It's primary telling was about agriculture, rural life, farming, bee-keeping, and husbandry. It was a tale of caring for the land and the animals -- therefore, the society that held together in peaceful production of human nourishment. Seems he hoped Octavian would see the benefits of this rather than a warring society… just finishing great wars. Times and civilizations have to change. Orpheus could no longer bring Eurydice back from the dead. Humanity has to live with that reality and create the best of times: times of "great growth."

From Virgil we leap forward to the Voltaire in the 18th Century. He said it was foolish to believe a God was causing earthquakes and pestilences because humanity deserved it. These were natural events and must be dealt with as such. He wrote a book CANDIDE that ended with the concept that we "must cultivate our gardens." We must take care of the propagation and cultivation of the "garden" within ourselves and in our land. Garden means vegetables and the holdings of "great growths" to nourish humanity with vitality and virtuous victories.

So here we have – VIRGIL-VOLTAIRE-VINEYARDS. Recalls the VICTORY Gardens of W War I & II times, when families were encouraged to grow their own gardens to ease the food strain of the wars and the show their independence and ability to do so – and as such would ensure Victory. Like a vine holding all together is VIRTUOUS VIRTUOSITY'S VIGILANCE and VERISIMILITUDE. This foray of "Vs" is in contrast to VIRTUAL, which is a computer simulation makes you think you are, physically, in a simulation of reality. There are even those who philosophize that we are "simulacra" in a "simulated" existence. This GOTMOL is based on our reality as truly real. -- All else in view – this is a time of the VIRUS, which is not Virtual. We must engage the Earth as our comrade for real in this *Astonishing Covenantal Embrace*, to have and to hold and "virtuously"cultivate our gardens to great growths. HAUT GRAND CRU!

VOILA! VIRTUE! VRAIE VERITE!

The meaning of life takes hold of us through the "truer sound" excellences of a virtuous challenge/ response with each day's "rise and shine." Today, we rise to face a different world with deeper-darker challenges. Today we must live a renewed shining from our candles of illumination. To use a major term of our day – we are *transitioning!* Old normals are out and may never make it back: certainly, not exactly. We'll dance with different steps and rhythms. This is evident in the world of those who are "spiritual without religion." Humanistic, Atheistic, and Free Thought societies are growing. The historical Jesus becomes a person of history and not a mythological, conspiracy theory figure of resurrection to immortality. People of whatever "people of transcendental faith" must agree to work beside those of "immanental faith." So much wrestling is so any arenas. We are severely challenged – physically, intellectually, economically, and spiritually. Getting all four on the nourishing ground of "great growths" is the quest --- with the vine of virtue, a great wine: like a fifth force, gathering all as one. The CLIMAT is not just a special, historical piece of vineyard ground for the greater growths of anyone's grapes or beliefs: it is the total Earth as Climat for the best of vintages of virtuous prosperity from humanity's holistic caress of the Earth and one another. Yes, working in scientific and virtuous harmony with one another and the earth describes succinctly and truly the Gracing Our Time's Meaning of Life. The Voila-Virtue-Vraie Verite Choir sings gracing praises from Virgil to Voltaire to….. Ventilators.

HALLEHOLDYOU! HALLEHOLDUS! HALLEHELDTRUE!

I expect most will intuit from the gist of the Hold their own list of gracings for their meaning of life. Finding and enhancing what holds for all is the unavoidable task. Unlike ages past – we are all technologically connected as never before. Such is our reality and it cannot be denied. With the aid of the sciences humanity will "increasingly" grasp the nature/laws/inevitability of how existence holds – to have and to hold – itself together and manifests the how – from TOE-GUT-HEAD – existences cohere to become their being – and sustain it. Alas, the BOD (Bard-Ovate-Druid) will feel and radiate the more to say from the more to know. Spiritually, the BOD, holistically, will carry into meaning the TGH. That's why I say "poetries" of a new spirituality. The 'Apo'kstrophes' of the future will be quite busy.

Is there a holding-holder beyond The Hold—some God beyond God? Quite honestly, I don't know, but it doesn't seem so in existence – except in the hold of thought. Seems the Cove came before the Rev and the Hold before God. And, so it is that some are beginning to say, philosophically, scientifically, and poetically, that THE HOLD is CONSCIOUSNESS ITSELF and the "neural network of the brain" mirrors the network of the galaxies. Of course, none speak of THE HOLD as I do. With all the new data coming from the sciences and the telescopes – such theories will have considerable "lift-off" as "human" time progresses. Should I persist a few years from now, I will give my commentary on where we are in this comprehension. [Currently, anyone can get into the swing of such theorizing with these two sources: the Vazza-Feletti analysis in Nautilis (The Strange Similarity of Neuron and Galaxy Networks) – and Lanza-Berman's "Biocentrism: How Life and Consciousness Are the Keys to Understanding the True Nature of the Universe."] I've some studying to do! However, just as I take a stand against any theory of human nature that doesn't begin with creaturely predation --- similarly, I take the stand in perplexed opposition to any TOE-GUT or FLOW theory that doesn't begin with the pervasive-primal HOLD that patterns existences. O! That Vraie Verite-Truer Sound.

What follows to help proclaim this GOTMOL, comes from SYMPATHIES: composed of excerpts from its two concluding apostrophes -- "In the Shining" and "Of Imminence and the Inevitable" – with an enhanced "eminence" this time. GOTMOL is our Eminence – which comes twixt the "imminent" and the "inevitable." An Eminence that holds in attack/flow (as in fencing lingo) twixt two "I's- -regardless of how thoughts of transcendent immortality come from our obviously Eminent Immanence mortality.

IN THE SHINING

Oh! I'll never forget the time we were immortals.
We would walk together in the shining sun as one,
Wore our raiment of radiance as blessing of the blest—
Woven-warm from thraldoms unbegun and ne'er undone:
Our vision-soaked eyes socketed in endless grace,
As primordial, imperishable pigments peered
Through us to blazonly spindle beauty's fiber.
Bold bathers, we, in life's overflow from death's cauldron.
Wonder-held in the embracing slide of galaxies,
We supped Earth's golden-cup-nectars thought for gods,
Felt in the majesty a music too magical to fray:
The singing of it flowing through us freshly free
As little brooks ripple over the stones of mountains.
…Oh! How I miss our mortal play, our sun-spun hold of hands.
Immortalizing thoughts grope to grasp the fabric of such fire:
Your fire fanned and launched to the lofty clouds
That bring us to dream and thirst for gentle rain.

AN EMINENCE MIDST IMMINENCES OF THE INEVITABLE

I might be able to boldly extend
The *engagement*, not letting the *en garde!*
Throw me into states of anxiety,
Even though I know my opponent,
Inevitably will win. After all,
This duel to the end, I take personally.
The death I'm holding-off, while neutral,
Has multitudinous moves and weaponry,
And my thrust and parry, while ever in *riposte*
With self-stylized *changement de Rythme* and *d'engagement,*
Are all my own dancing moves, in courtship with life – where
To keep the big band playing and the choir singing,
The constant *affair d'honneur* is one's own *affair de Coeur.*
Before the passionless inevitable, Life's a dancing fencer!
This match-up seeks to perform as eminence within immanence
Ah! The *touche* of *assault! Salut* to *Salut!*
The command to eminence is clear:
En garde! Presentation! Engagement!
Marche!.....ATTAQUE AU FER!---[Such is Athena's fight for wisdom!]

THE GIST FROM THE MIST

Well, GOTMOL should speak a code – some most graspable gist of the tale as told. Recall the HEAD with its BOD (inclusive of GUT & TOE, and all component-operatives of the inner INTERSTITIUM and outer creations of EPITOFITME.) Briefly: Hold Everything And Dance! Yes, and GRACE can be cast as the *Grand-cru Rhymed Astonishing Covenantal Embrace*. There is a holding capacity/magic to creation that sustains its embrace to form the rose, the rhino, the Rolls Royce, and the rhymer. Scientists are still searching for that "gluon-axion, etc." that causes the coherence that forms matter out of existence's ever-imminent total annihilation potential. After all, something has a holding pattern at work – nothing has nothing. Alas, IAM THAT IAM rises to flame and glory from the Syntangoion dance of the contraries. See it as HOME that sustains between the Ship's Passage with Cargo in the HOLD and the Castle's stronghold, KEEP, as the place of last refuge and defense. The Grace of being at Home between Defense and Destiny.

This is clear: there is a holding manifestation that keeps existences together so that trees and bees emerge as ACEs. GRACES! And the gracings of our time's meaning of life are those "holdings" that balance our lives as we are living and that make us feel at home. We can't see this --- call it the FIFORONAT – fifth force of nature. Behold the image of pyramids below: my best, for now, illustration of this invisible alchemic absolute adhesive.

We see the four sides of the pyramid, but not the fifth dimension, which is the base from which the four arise and are held and grounded. This pyramid (from my website) was chosen to represent, the seven layers, the seven sounds of breathing in the five breaths of the QUINTETOION – the fifth dimension of which is the HOLD which is the base. Thus, five sides. In breathing, between each breath is THE HOLD – that FIFORONAT at work.

I put it beside the pyramids of Egypt as its distinctive layers represent active breathing and the magical threshold of seven-fold. All aligned with concrete creations – Egypt and beyond -- which would not be (not hold) without THE HOLD. Spiritually, HOME is the GRACE that holds us in place midst life's defenses and destinies: twixt its ultimate passing and ubiquitous passage. When Home, we are held with THE HOLD of feelings and thoughts of a transcendent well-being. Indeed, an Eminence within Immanence the wrestles the imminent to release the transcendent. Amazing! From that which holds – pops-out the transcendent. Just like that dancing-candle-flame of IAM in the Syntangoion. The rising-holding pyramids come from that same emergence and symbolize it. Perhaps ancient Egyptians found that out.

These pyramids show how the fifth dimension, fifth side, fifth instrument of breathing --- is unseen but the foundation of what arises. The seven layered marble one I can hold in my hand; lift it to show the unseen base, the fifth side/instrument – just as I can pull-up the grass to show its roots. THE HOLD is that pervasive "something" that holds everything to evolve to be what it is. These pyramids and the small one each have their being because of THE HOLD, which is pervasive in all that exists in order to exist. This is the "ground of being-grass-roots" of humanity's "New Being" of Meaning. GOTMOL is within and not beyond: life-beyond-death is lived now. This has been humanity's greatest challenge since the beginning…no matter what one may religiously believe. The Hold is always time's-eternal-now-wisdom of the New Being…as the ANSWER BEING. – Humanity has to hold on to what HOLDS US& PLANET together as harmoniously as possible for all. Grasping THE HOLD's GOTMOL is in the grasp of all. This calling-chorus Graces Our Time's Meaning of Life.

Howsoever dark is dark-matter, we are the songs of The Dawn On The Lawn.

The concert of the Syntangoion and 'Apo'kstropes', as pervasive performance, I must display again. Remember, we are talking about gracing our time's meaning of life: our purpose being to enhance/ comprehend life's purpose for our purpose. That middle candle, held as it holds, emerges from the contrasting forces of existence. This that holds for us – in doing so -- uses the holding form-to-function/function-to-form process of the entire universe of existence. A universe that comes not from nothing, or unknown something, but from its holding. THE HOLD! Because of THE HOLD we are it's offspring as THE CONSCIOUS HOLDERS. In our Earth world there is great randomness as in the universe that we can now see. With all the galaxial holds as stars and planets and asteroids, etc. – there are constant destructions and helter-skelters out there. Surely, it appears that the concert of Earth-Sun and its Species – amidst all we can now see – has been the result of that random-hold/ hold of random - power potential.

Is there a purpose to the universe of existence and us? If there is it would seem that it would have to be grasped by some concept of THE HOLD WITHIN RANDOMNESS AND POWERFUL ENERGIES. In other words, life in death[A]death in life. That [A} is the 'Apo'kstrophes' – whether one is poet-scientist-philosopher-spiritualist-thinker-etc. – who is trying to describe and sound-out that which is obviously there is some fashion – but is invisible: namely that which holds things together to become what they can become and persist so until they no longer hold together and are gone. It's a tough perplexing puzzle. I don't have the feeling of a Deity-Divinity behind it all – but THE HOLD is an intriguing and challenging reality. We do covenant with it and in that respect ancient religions and mythologies were aware of the need to establish "proper-to-prosper" relationships with this power at work everywhere. Because Humanity has used religion/dogma to as a power over others in a detrimental fashion, and as a power over the evolving mind – I do not find such religion as the answer, no matter how much it is a reflection of our human need to feel/believe one is HELD by what HOLDS. That that feel/believe need finds and enhances its gracings --- is the meaning of our life. How it has happened we are very very far from comprehending ----if ever …….. before we and this planet are gone.

We are Odysseans ever on the journey home -- having arrived time-after-time, to clean-house with each new revelation. When I hold a thought, your image with my eyes, a flower in my hand as I pet the dog - I know THE HOLD is more than poetry and metaphor. It's a daily, every moment, reality. Forward Ho!!!

ECRASEZ L' INFAME

Voltaire (1694-1778) supposedly crafted this phrase around 1759 –"crush the infamous(loathsome) thing." It was his watchword signature phrase-sound-directive for the rest of his life. He was, of course, referring to the power of the Catholic Church within the State of France. He was especially in contention (as a Deist) with the Church's calling earthquakes and plagues the punishing acts of the Church's God. His was a strident call for the separation of church and state. A reported quote from him: "Those who can make you believe in absurdities can make you commit atrocities." Catholic priests tried to get a deathbed confession. He waved them aside saying "Let me die in peace."

The Catholic church had a long involved history in France. In 1231 CE, the Inquisition was initiated which tortured and killed those deemed heretics. This suppression heresy was reinstated in 1542 CE to combat Protestantism. This continued for 700 years until the last execution in1826. Along with the Inquisition was the sale of Indulgences to raise money for the church and for people to reduce afterlife punishments, get free admission to heaven, and be protected from future sins. This began in 1095 CE and was abolished in 1567.

I've reviewed this history, because the separation of church and state is a growing issue in the USA. Along with this is the recent development of conspiracy theories and various denials of science and climate change. The Tsunami symbol has been used to dramatize the growing reality of climate threats and crises on Planet Earth and our industrial involvements of making it so. Add to this the COVID-19 pandemic and the attempt from some evangelical religionists to say its cause by God as punishment, etc. The issue that Voltaire faced that brought forth his famous "delete the stupidities"(my updated version) – is resurfacing in the World and the USA in particular. The cosmologists and their telescopes and equations are showing a universe of chaos rather than of God: pointless rather than purposeful. The battle has just begun between science and the religionists. The Trump era has inflamed this circumstance by accepting that he is God's Chosen to lead the world and that has a Religious Advisor who visits the Throne of God. All of this and the ease of floating crazy theories and call for violence via the internet and phones in every pocket. This midst the growing awareness that we are moving rapidly to a systemic new normal of humanity and Earth. The philosophers/physicists are forging new theories all the time now as technology produces more data daily.

The new watchphrase is something like Cherish the Earth-Human Caress. The context is this: climate change/crises – pandemic contagion – separation of church and state – creating and administering the "shots" that control this and future contagions—stopping the denials of science – advancing education of these and their allied realities as they affect human wellness, justice, and longevity. Many gracings will be the same – dogs-family-gardens-music-love-hope, wine, apples, etc. New ones are at work to structure the Meaning of Life. OUR TIME is forwarding with a limp, but will gain traction and HOLD TRUE to itself on this new trail. It will be a Global fusing of Earth and Humanness as never before. That task is quite clear as are the benefits and gracings.

As I write about THE HOLD becoming more of a spiritual-daily-human reality, I've been remind that from the beginning of the birth of the human species

(all species actually), each creature has been HELD with total care awareness in THE HOLD OF THE WOMB, before being birthed into the world – where that feeling of being held in the hold is continuously sought to be regained in THE HOLD OF LIFE WITH DEATH beyond the womb. If we didn't know it before, technology's global voice tells us about deaths everywhere in everyway everyday. The developing gracings are forming from the sciences-arts and earthborne spirituality rather than religion and its dogmas. More and more, it seems, the meaning of life will be fashioned and held Earth-Immanently-Here rather than After Earth Transcendentally.

Humanity must work cooperatively to comprehend and control the rising tsunami. The voices from Virgil to Voltaire to todays Ventilators are crying-singing for virtuous victory. GOTMOL means work and commitment. That "G" is also for GLOBALING GALLOPS OF GREEN GRACINGS GALORE!! This GONG sound's not to be heard like "g" in "dogmatic," or "G" in "God." And the more we hear/heed the sounding call of GROCEREIES – the more this GOTMOL is comprehended.

GLOBAL GARDEN OF GREENS
AND GROCERIES

Today, so many use the phrase "In God We Trust" as a divisive dogma. Since the Far-Right Populism of the Trump era, the police cars, local and county, in my part of WV have this painted on them. Why, one must ask, did they not paint "In Justice We Trust" on these "Justice" vehicles? The answer is clear and Voltaire would cry aloud ERASEZ L'INFAME! The attempt to manipulate The Separation of Church and State in an increasingly secular-scientific world is integral to the denial of these realities as they are re-shaping, re-gracing, our concept of existence. A new era of Eartharian Enlightenment is emerging through cosmology-coronavirus-covenantal-climate-world of cultures and AI consciousness. POANSWER – Poetries of a New Spirituality We R are on the increase to fill the void of declining power of religious institutions. Recently, the Pope gave credence to the LGBTQ community within Catholicism. Is a woman's right to an abortion next? Humanity is learning that "spirituality" is not contingent on such versions of human compassion: is, indeed, inclusive of them.

As I finish this GOTMOL the world is in a worsening grip of the coronavirus. Labs are on the brink of a vaccine that has worldwide potential. We'll know more as 2020 comes to an end. Again, this is not the work of a traditional deity on either end – the infection or the vaccine. Both dimensions are the work of Earth and Human potentials in concert. The earth produces the tsunamis and we the vaccines – plus increasing knowledge of how to control the infections, tsunamis, and produce ever-more effective vaccines. In every instance, I perceive THE HOLD at work in all existences and our growing awareness – from stars to apples -- that we must know and nourish what holds true with the greatest hope and promise for our existence. To be engaged with the love and caress of that destiny is to be ennobled by a new spirituality of Humanness and Earth singing in new choirs of Global Belongsong. Rings True! Holds True! Sings Real! That which holds life: not from some ancient scripture that never telescoped a galaxy or a black hole or felt the needle of a vaccine – but the gracings of life as lived in the context of OUR TIME!

There is nothing more real and symbolic of humanity's ageless covenant with the earth than – OUR GLOBAL GARDEN OF GREENS AND GROCERIES. All species have to eat to live. I would not consider the hungry person "well" should they prefer to chose belief in a deity over nourishing food to eat – right in front of them. Alas, we were predators long before we learned to cultivate our gardens and produce "groceries." In this, is the meaning of "my-our-time" motivation to change the title of Reverend to Covernend and Rev. to Cove.

Still, even in the world of liberal religion, no one even wants to discuss this change. Ah! The EXTOLLINGS of such have both the "toll" to pay of passage across bridges to tomorrow and the "toll" of bells ringing the praises of the journey. When it come to TR-U-TH, we all must find and secure the "U" within. Time both takes its toll, makes a stand, and rings its bells. All as of these three: Liberty-Buddhist-Ancient… and the ship's bell ringer. The crack in Liberty tolls the Toll. The

Buddhist Arch tolls THE HOLD. The ancient bell tolls the Choir of Praise since the beginning of human soundings. Bells, like the human voice "songed", when "gonged" have a sustained holding resonance of tonality -- which manifests The Hold of the Human-Earthen Duet. The Sound of Profound. Ring It! GONG!

WHAT RINGS TRUE HOLDS TRUE--
WHAT HOLDS TRUE RINGS TRUE

! EXCLAMATION POINT !

THE HOLD is rather magical and sparingly comprehensible. But it's there in the colored feathers of birds, acorn of oaks, pages of books, and stars of galaxies. Things become what they are to ever be what they are because of THE HOLD OF THE HELD WE BEHOLD. Wind turbines are a good example. I've no "elegant" formulae or gut-toe theories of STANDARD-FIXED-CYCLICAL-STRING or BIOENTRIC universes. Well, I've added the HEAD which is the force holding any existences in unison be they trees or theories, particles or strings: and, as always, observer and observed. And the deeper we can see into the workings of nature the play of how our consciousness does its "holding" finds common ground with all other existent's "bonds" and their holding patterns. And, so it is we can make cars, computers, cathedrals, communities --- and love. Even make it seem like consciousness and intelligent design are absolute and everywhere in every why of anything at all. But there is much-much randomness. Today, we can see ever so much more now that ever into the universe and in our Eartharian existence. A tsunami like COVOID-19 can just out of the blue and destroy multitudes and natural catastrophes as fires-hurricanes-tornadoes-floods-drought in random concert with climate change and crises all over the globe.

Let's say there is some form of Deity and I, as billions upon trillions of quadrillions of others before me, have a chance to question why creation is as it is before I pass-on to the "fantasies of immortality." I would begin by saying I' m really "pissed" that things "blessed" go as they do. Why did you build predation/killing into all species and why did you build randomness into all events??? And, of course, all these result in horror, death, randomness, and chaos. Granted there is procreation and prosperity, but why is death and chaos the means to get there???Why no care and compassion that "all" such beautiful and hopeful creatures should not experience/fear the horror of "roadkill? Where's the "good" the "justice" the "grace" and the "love" in such a scenario of censored sentience? And, lastly, why are the religions that believe and worship you as "dog-god-matic" cause so much violence in the world? I can hear the first-only response -- as the eternal cry-out-directive from the statistically resonant graceless-gong of gone -- NEXT! NEXT! ("Le suivant, le suivant!" The ending of Jacques Brel's song "Au suivant," about a virgin young soldier's encounter with a "military provided" prostitute-brothel. The command coming from The Commanding Officer —NEXT! A metaphor of learning and growing-up. Always Something!) We humans are ever re-choiring GOTMOL to transcend just being NEXT. -- SOBEUS! HALLEHOLDUS!!!!!!!

AS THE CHOIR'S ON HOLD

As the Choir rests from all this singing-chanting-exclaiming of proclamation and purpose – it becomes clear as blue sky following the storm that the big "G" in GOTMOL has Grandeurs of Global Green in its Gracings. It is the GREENING that captures our soundings now to compose our gardens anew. Indeed, to protect and sustain all the lovely gracings of life on Earth that we know so well, we must go as green as can be. The gigafires, hurricanes, tornadoes, floods, droughts, earthquakes, temperature increases, specie harm/ extinctions, and virus contagions, etc. – are crying-out-loud for us to GREEN OUR BELONGSONG. Sing-Sang-Sung!! Sound those "G's" as in Green-Grace & Grocereies!!!

Gracings old and gracings new must be protected and sustained – HELD -- by a vigorous and deeply spiritual greening covenant of humanity and earth. The earth and our societies are full of upheaval and change – yet the time is, as if presently ON HOLD, waiting for humanity's response to compose the new music knowing the world will never be the same. The Paris Accords of 12/2015 symbolize the grasp of the future now—with COVID-19 -- that all nations and peoples must aspire to. It's the Age for the SAGES – Sciences Advancing Green's Eureka Songs! -- Wind Turbines! Electric cars! Plant based Burgers! Replacements for plastics! Eurekas All! Belongsongs All! Gratitudes of Gratefulnesses!! So much to love.

And so it is that I end this GOTMOL with the hope of SAGES and many more GREENING EUREKAS! –GREUKS! It must be so if we are to continue with GRACING OUR TIME'S MEANING OF LIFE. The color and constitution of the new, inescapable, normal is GREEN and today's ultimate GRACE is the Growth of Our Greening. Actually GLACIER GREEN! – OK! Time to stand-up, grab hold, ring the bells, and start singing the new verses to OUR SONG! -- Talk of our Blue Planet will continue, but it's Greenness is a Growing Grace.

This GOTMOL needs a period. Some twenty-five years ago I found, antiquing, the following Crystal Ball Marble (2 inches in diameter) to rub occasionally to see the future. I look at it in my study every day. An exclamation's point it is! Yet a proclamation! O! Passage Owl of Epiphanic Tang! Behold the Challenges! Innovations for Hope's elation!

GOTMOL's GOT THE BALL – HOLD ON!

PASSAGES OF EPOCHAL MENSES

EXCLAMATION POINTS & POEMS OF PERIODS

Just tracing the gracings of the secret-hidden-obvious forces of existence for renewed life.

Michio Kahn said in his *Physics of the Future* (Anchor, 2011, p. 11): "Today, we have become choreographers of the dance of nature . . . by 2100, we will make the transition to being masters of nature." --- "Masters" in my sense means Covenanters of what Holds to be Held. Yes, we will do the TANGO in the Syntangoion. Alas, dancers in partnership with the Earth. Our alchemical magic on this planet has been as choir director and choreographer – singer and dancer: builders of gateways through challenges. ACES in the HOLDS! And death ever on the horizon. Now, as this GOTMOL is concluding, there are three COVID-19 vaccines ready for distribution by year's end. This epitomizes the human-nature dance and how we use the holding dimensions to find what holds true. This, of Our Time, shows clearly how we continue to face our-nature's challenges and attain the gracings of our time and meaning of life. Our Covenantally Inspired Destiny! So, as a symbol of so much that holds-rings-sings true – I hold this Green Marble, back&forth, in the palms of my hands and sense a resonance of hope beyond my own grasp – and GOTMOL's continuing presence in human life. Our Mastercraft "mastering" our beholdings of thresholds that hold true as "gracings" of our passage with the "ring-true" Bell-Choirs of the surest HELDS of THE HOLD.

Such Gracings come as the Blessings of Groceries.!
Virgil&Voltaire keep crying so above the vicissitudes!

EPILOGUE AS PROLOGUE

And so -- a not so new and yet ever so – awareness gasps for air in the delivery room. Humanity has been there so many-many times – as the hold of the womb is released into the randomness of the world's potential of holding patterns and the individual's quest for Strategic Sustainable Stability in those patterns. Emerson, in his essay *Self Reliance,* said "Prayer is the contemplation of the facts of life from the highest point of view. It is the soliloquy of a beholding of the jubilant soul." Ah, to understand the "jubilant soul" beholding. This "prayer" reminded me of a poem – "Paradiso" in *Altarpieces,* composed in 2011 after two-stented heart attack. Still alive! Another ascent from Purgatory! What's next!

Ahh! The struggle with COVID-19's pandemic tsunamic contagion. We must hold on and hold up with what holds new-true to do! That "exclamation point" seems a fit conclusion to GOTMOL. I see it in the back cover of Liberty holding the torch of freedom high and victorious. We must not let go!

PARADISO

This time . . . .
Oozes in cantos,
Spongy like Spring mud,
Boots full of Kairos:
Clodhopper heaven.

Stomping-up
Old paradigm hill
In Minerva's gale,
High on cracking sun:
Soul soar-sore at the top.

Ah, this coming home.
Rest Odysseus,
Be home with your dreams.
Fire the castle hearth.
Boots off. Rock a while.

Still, nostril's flair.
Steeds in the blood churn:
Sweat beads, glistening
In twilight. Peak's glow!
Something oozes yet

In what's left of the sun . . . . . .

SOBEUS

Perhaps OUR SONG is but as "gracenotes" in the catastrophic grandeur of existence.

! HALLEWEHOLDDON !

AFIRADAPO'S PROPHET'S ANSWER TO 5 G

FROM GLISTENINGS TO THE DAWN'S
BALM ON THE LAWN

SOUL – So, dear Prophet what to you have to say from your Fireflies At Dawn Poiesis and *Songs Of Dawn's Balm On The Lawn* belongsong about the 5G – Fifth Generation of technology that makes technology connections stronger and greater and ever-more-so? O! *SO-DA-BA-O-LA!*

PROPHET – It will more greatly manifest that "magical something" called The Hold and how We-R HELD. That tech-generation will truly activate the now-generation I've termed GEN-i-US. Indeed, it will require an advanced Genius Consciousness to get things right.

SOUL – Given the various Gracings of our time's meaning of life in this new world and given the brightest Glistenings sparking from our Song Of Dawn On The Lawn singalongbelong "five-beat" song of SODABAOLA with HALLEWEHOLDON's 5 beats – what 5G words of wisdom have you to share?

PROPHET – As you know by now, we've been dwelling in the realm of the Quintetoion of breathing and the FIFORNAT data from dark matter through the fine-tuned-structure of the universe: and various poetic/portends of the quintessential 3D world of destiny-death-divinity – natural to our earthly existence. But beyond theories, statistics, and flights of fancy – there are real glistenings sparking from The Dawn's Balm On The Lawn. This 5G holds the gist of Golden Mean's Most Supernatural Glory to include with God & Gaia:

GREEN PLANET – GALAXIES – GLACIERS – GARBAGE – GROCERIES

And, if GOTMOL were to pick one word of these -- and any others under consideration that would manifest the firmest grasp of what holds the most for our thresholding-beholding and that nourishes every corner and play of our ACE in the deal – the choice is easy. It's the ever-dominate GAIA-GARDEN-GRACINGS-GREEN-GOODNESS – in a tri-sound word --

!!! GROCERIES !!!
[ACE Groceries and all else will manifest holding patterns of health-truth-justice-beauty.]
--Includes Wine and Vaccines—

CODA

That this GOTMOL is an imperfect document does not disturb me. For instance, physicists are now discussing black holes as manifests of String Theory. Black Holes are no longer the great swallowers of all that comes close – star-stuff never to be seen again—with just a little Hawking's radiation to get free. Now, they are "fuzz balls" made-up of collapsed and gathered strings. And they belch-up what they've swallowed! Ah! Black Holes are still a mystery. The universe is still a mystery. GOTMOL is saying/singing that what holds on this planet (so that things/species/events can become what they are and continue to be that – personally/creaturely and as progeny until death do us part) is deeply kin to what holds existence together. A hold that is attuned with a sync and a tang to what holds all existence to be as it is --- whether Black Holes are unregurgitant swallowers to annihilation, or Fuzz Balls that keep throwing-up existences back into its own face --- so to speak. --- So, GOTMOL, howsoever imperfect, is doggedly on track and stride up the mountain of evidences and epiphanies. On the way, we daily sip our own elixir of Eartharian life within the magic of THE HOLD: armed with its what holds true to truth and musical notes we each learn that loudly sing OUR SONG's HALLEHOLDME HALLEHOLDYOU. So, there is a real sense of being on the right track up the right mountain. Our walking stick -- an Augur's Staff. Our Consciousness an Astonishing Covenantal Embrace of Humanity & Nature. All trails lead to the grocery store. Amazing the hunger and poverty on this planet. Our SingAlongSong – The GOTMOL HALLEHOLDUS HALLEWEHOLDON CHORUS. -- *HALLEGOTMOL!*

[P.S. – Don't forget that events caused by various catastrophes and climate warming -- utilize and work from the same structure-dynamics of this Universal Hold as do we. Mosquitos, such as the deadly *Aedes aegypti* and bats, generally, carry multiple viruses to humans – and work from that same holding process built into nature, whereby coherences form to produce things to be what they are. Globally, viruses are on the move more and we are more vulnerable. The Earth and Humanity are at a critical turning point. Vaccines are created from the same processes that allows contagions to manifest. – The scientific- spiritual/cultural-poetical are as teams to grasp and work with the hold of things – and within our human world. GOTMOL has to get really real. The good, the bad, the ugly and the great -- use the same tuned constants of existence. We are perhaps the first epoch of humanity with the sciences and history to realize this -- on a much grander-galactic scale than ancient beliefs could even guess -- and the necessity to proceed accordingly. The coronavirus is yelling at us --- The loss of loved ones teaches us of THE HOLD's sacred memory and the caressing HELD of HOME, if we but listen and walk gracefully our lawn midst the glistens and balms of the dawn. I concluded *If I'm Ever To Hold You Again* (see MOM, p. 83) as follows:

> *Oh! To just hold you as Planet & Air,*
> *Inseparable holding-pattern, like Space & Time.*
> *We as Earth & Sky in that HOLD as one:*
> *That Keep of Life & Death ever-Held as Home!*
> MDOK – 12/2020

APPENDIX I

__BEYOND A VERY BLEARY QUERY THEORY OF Y Y Y__
__TO FORGE A PURGE OF PURGATORIOS__ -- Here's __an APE--Autobio Poetic Essay__
__An AFIRADAPO ALPHA APE—A DAWN'S BALM ON THE LAWN ARIA__
__SUNG BEYOND -- W H Y -- to refrains of a WISER HUMANITY'S YAY!!!__

Why are so Many Y-Y-Ys of Whys not Wise to Rise to Sunny Skies?
How did we become so wise to surmise with & past so many Whys!?
Why's Y the ending of many ways we say "NAY? Y!?"
Every Day By Day has a Nay-Say-May-Day that Lays the Way.
Our often to speak of it is to squeak it so weak and bleak . . . it leaks.
Barely a therefore from the wherefores of the here-to-fores.
Week after Week! Story after Story! Y-This! Y-That! Why do we exist?

Purgatorio Scenarios --- looking for a Way-Up & Out!

We're so caught-up in many queries of WHY-WHY- LIVE2DIE?
Something has to re-story this Nay-factory's Other-Worldly-Glory!
A more sun-shiny scope of hope with rope to cope past Worldly-Sorry!
A cozy-homey clime where our rhyming rimes true and on time!
HALLE! Okay! Okay! Okay! Make My Day! Have A Good Day! OLE!
Then go *open-the-often* of every way to stay the nay -
Having had enough of being drought-tough in the rough,
But still powered to go choral with our We-R lovers-frolic
Singing ever-clearer the music in showers of clover-logic.

Time to gather warm at the wild world's hold
Of flower and grower and knowers bold!
Be the behold -- as ever told – no matter how cold the cold!
Ahh! The clever seasoner enfolds a fold's hold – howsoever!
Yes! Just apply over "any-Y" the ans-wer-flo-wer-po-wer of WE -- R !!

We made it, can proclaim it, can do it. Scroll & Roll it!
Talk it & Walk it -- with never a forever NAY full of "Ys"
To compromise our Earthen Prize -- the sun's rise on the Wise --
That eternal-now-song of dawn's-balm-on-the-lawn as heaven's leaven.

O! Galaxies in the scopes! O! Antelopes on the slopes!
Q! Elation-revelation! Our long for home belongsong
Sings our "A-OKAY" and our grace sounds of ACE,
From our *Astonishing Covenantal Embrace,*
Twixt the ever "for and aft" of those Y's of --- "baby-(fly-by)-bye!"
So comes our Come & Become & Begone!! Me-Me-One Done!
Why these in a universe that doesn't cry? Or Sigh! Or answer Why!
O! to rid every daily bleary query of NAY's YYYs – with……….

YAY! YAY! YAY! Hurray! Be a Wiser Humanity's Yay!
O! Fire of Firefly. O! Utter of Butterfly. O! Honks of Honkers in Flight!
It's "A-OKAY" to play our ACE every Day:
Your long to Belong rhyming its Gong, singing its sang-song!
As they say: the lay of the say plays the say of the lay.
O! The whys can be Alpha-AUM-YogA wise to caress Aria's of "A."
ALLELUIA! Aufklarung! Atonement! 'Apo'kstrophes'! *ACAPELLA!*

Surprise! Surprise! Open Your Eyes! Hold-On! Ride the Tide!
Mind Your Mind! Wow Your TAO! AUM Your Agnst!
Sound your BreathSong's Hold through Random's Storms!
Ascend! Aspire! Attract! Do the Open Often [A]Often Open . . .
So Blessings Bloom in the Caress of Rain, the Duress of Pain.

Hoist Your Alpha Voice&Noise from your Inner Poise! -- (O I O!)
Cry – AAAHHHH//AAAAHHH!!! Be ever born again! – (O i O!)

Whatever the ending of beginning in whatever inning of singing --
Go! Seek a peek and sneak a speak. Sweep the deck of the leaks!
Dawn's A Balm On the Lawn! New Ports are calling as we speak!
Sing It! Be an "Alpha-A-OKAY!" --a "Brilliant-Jubilant"
Of any totally Alpha -- " AHHH-HAAA" – ANS-WE-R's writ.

Time to Rime Mine in the WE-R of Ours and One's Own Time.
Why Not? Why not – wise-up and rise-up from Pugatorios
To the Paradiso Prize of one's own and our -- Eternity in Time?

ETERNITY-DIVINITY-HUMANITY-SANITY-DEITY-INFINITY-LONGEVITY, etc.
With so many ITS WITH "Y's" past asking -- the wiser are daily-riser basking!

Sunrise-Sunshine-Sunset. Let there be light!
SONGS OF DAWN'S BALM ON THE LAWN.
BLESSINGS OF BIRDS ON THE WING.
RHYMES OF FAMILY WITH BEAUTY-DUTY.
THE GARDEN'S GROCERIES OUR HONORARY DEGREE!
DO THE SUPER IN SUPERNATURAL NATURALLY.
Halleholdus! JOIN THE CHOIR & DO YOUR SING. *Halleholdyou!*
BE A YAY! OKAY!?! FULLY HERE TODAY! IT'S OKAY!
MAKE COVID SAY COVENATALLY INSPIRED DESTINY!
AND YOU'RE ON YOUR BELONGSONG WAY HOME!

! HALLEHOLDWE -- HALLEHOLDON !

Remember, throughout GOTMOL, the daily truth -- that the SUPERNATURAL is the superlative, absolute best of being natural here and now (not other-worldly). The more our lived reality of THE HOLD (Wholly Earthly Angels of WE!) becomes technological/medical/spiritual -- and WE planet-vulnerable-victorious -- the more our connection, covenant, caress with nature and ourselves must become SUPER. Of course, this rhymes/times with SUPPER (our need to "breakfast&fastbreak" past "no free lunch"). This rhymes proudly with the UPPER-UT-MOST of SUPERHUMAN—those super gracings, nourishments, and deepest depths of people-planet wellness. That UT has an inescapable ***Ubiquitous Tang.*** Here are three UT words – CAFETERIAAHHA! --FARMWORKERRRR! – *VACCINATIONS!!!!!* **–That apple in Marilyn's upreaching-grasping, hold-in-the-hand, symbolizes the UTmost of UT. Ah! The Dedication!**

[Note: The date of this entry is 12/21/20. Just learned about SUPER AGERS – a category which must include me since I've no Dementia or Alzheimer symptoms, so far. At issue: the health of the brain and the requirement of genes that fend-off protein build-up in the brain. Proteins described as such: tau protein tangles and beta protein amyloid plaques. Thought: time for humanity to become a SUPER AGER – and keeps its GEN-i- US sharp and currently focused. Thought: there are Tangles&Plaques everywhere in the world's populace today. Perhaps a new metaphor- TAP – to include science denials and conspiracy theory susceptibility. Howsoever comprehended, Earth & Covenantal Humanity (EACH) are at a pivotal time in history of both planet and its people (species, too, as 161 or more are endangered). It is a time when – the Reasoned Reality Renaissance of science, justice, and compassion join forces to work and harvest the most fertile fields of destiny. The presiding prescient Faith – to be in that which Holds so all wonders/groceries are held in place, in mind, and in every heart-beat, breath of life, and purpose of being.]

<u>GOTMOL ALERT!</u>

This book concludes at a time when stats from the coronavirus are as follows: 76.83 million infected worldwide/1.69 million have died --- 17.84 million infected in USA/317,000 have died --- and countings continue in all categories as an Xmas surge is expected. Also, new MUCOVAs (Mutant Coronavirus Variants) are emerging just as two viable vaccines are being delivered to millions. Conflicts will flare as "in science-justice-health-care we trust" takes rein of our gallop: clashes of technologies, religion, cultures, races, economies, poverty, hunger, climate crises, countries, etc. will happen. COVID & MUCOVAs – elevate both science and vulnerability. Religion's "salvation" will be greatly compromised; political plays to keep its power will be loud. Secular (Sacral-Scientific) Humanism will increase. Church & State issues increase. Civil unrest will join economics, workforce, and educational restructuring as the, restless, new normal evolves to Quintessential HOLDING PATTERNS (QUHOPATS) that WorkWorldwideWellnessWonders of We-R (WWWWW). The world is under duress and it must have leaders whose "Lives" exemplify and naturally enhance the "inspired destiny" of the ACE Gracing Our Time's Meaning Of Llife. Time to hold on -- be held with what holds best -- singing our song.

That **"H"** in front of Alleluia is for The HOLD--EACH of our gracenotes (all inner-variances included), as we, get a better (Super-Ager) grasp the graces/glories/goodnesses of the future of humanity as it is being re-designed, re-destined, and re-born. (Re-voluitions of re-ligion, too!)(Portents of Poetic Potencies on Purpose will Prevail!) Be Pre-ppppp-ared!!!!!

BEHOLD THE ROUSING *REALITY CHOIR'S* SINGING OF *HALLEHOLDON!*
BEHOLD LIBERTY'S LIFTED TORCH OF IDENITY AND COMPASSION!
HEAR ANEW "OUR SONG" FOR "OUR TIME"

! HALLEHOLDUS !

[Tonight, the cosmic conjunctjon of Saturn and Jupiter – the first since 800 years ago. An event said to augur great changes in civilization. O-KAIROS. Scientifically the time is ripe. – mdok 12/21/20 – As I note this 1/12/2021 -- The Trumpistas have brought violent insurrection to our Capitol (more to come) and over 4000 people are dying a day from COVID-19 in USA.]

APPENDIX II

Another Chest-Thumping Jungle-Bellowing APE --
From Swinging on Vines of Fantasy to Daily Rounds on the Ground of Being

THIS STRANGE TIME OF THE STAY-WITH OF ANGELS

I wake to it everyday -- knowing someday I'll not awake,
Yet existence, they telescope, will galaxy-on some zillions of years.
O Existences not alive as we! O Thrive of Life – beyond the "Stuff" of It!
       But out of it -- but to not be -- **but** out of it.
       O! To be more! Many thanks for our itty-bit of IT.
The news is full of people dying – tsunamis-pandemics-accidents --
Of predators-preying-- doing, dying things to selves and others --
And upon this solar planet and its species:
Policing and politics –even poetries --
Flashing their sirens so often after the fact. O! 2020!/2021!
       Suddenly so lonely! I can't meet with Thees &Thous,
       Breathing the same air as the virus,
       Or sit a spell with others as a usual Us.
       Strange time! Midst Many Minuses – but still a Plus!
       Someday a statistic with no notable fuss.
Many gather in churches – out of fear, or Love, or Salvation's
Visions of a somewhere Deity's Otherness place
Beyond Science's servings of Daily grace --
All – expecting a planet's destiny . . . to erase without a trace.
Many, like me, are stay-at-home-bound,
Awaiting the vaccine to stabilize the ground;
Free our feet, again, to run around.
Still, the Great Cry howsoever yelled aloud,
Or rumbled deep within hearts living proud --
       Is **Salvation.** Save Me and Us! US so Earthly!
       Let us live our planetary lives here. Fully! Lovingly!
       I wake to it everyday. EVERYDAY!
Come! My-Stay-With-Me-Angels for my say-song of the way! Stay!
Keep alive the living!– O! Paradises of yesteryear! Stay! Love again! Guide again!
Today, biodiversity-genesis outplays biblical eternity/genesis.
Global&Galaxial gallops over Gospel. Species over Scripture.
Spirituality evolves a new Earthliness -- The Holy a new Wholism.
The Holy Grail's an Earthen Pail that holds water -- a Wellness that replenishes!
I'M NOT A LONE STRANGER TO THIS STRANGEST OF TIMES:
DreamTime mixed with DyingTime. Justice for all -- over Gods for some.

Daily Grace of Groceries before Gaggles of Gospels.

Grub & Hugs over Tales of Afterlife Eternal. Staying Alive!

Magic and Tragic ever rhyming-scheming to unveil the Truth!

The random universe in tandem with our home-alone planet.

Again! Again! As ever! The Chorus, back and forth, weaving!

AWAKE! There's a Tell in the Take! A Life in the Strife,

Where the Magical outshines the Tragical – Groceries the Gross

The Existential outclassing the Statistical. O! Liturgy of the Hungry!

Immanence an immediacy over transcendence.

Science & Religion wedded! Me and the Pope vaccinated – 1/2021!

O! EarthenPatriots with that longing for Angelic Spring again! Evermore!

THAT STAY-WITH-ME EMBRACE OF WINGS FROM EARTH'S PARADISE!

Those memories/images of when all was a belongsong's hamony

Loved ones, pets, hearth-homes all alive in the paradise of family- in human time.

O! Those SHOALS OF WONTSUNODI! O! How they Stay With Me…With US.

Music that ever plays from their Stay as a Winged-Embrace of Meaning.

Come Home My Lovely Spring! My Summer Soul has too long been Wintering!

    O to hold in hand its flowers -- its petal's soft upon the lips.

    O dreams of dew freshed by *The Angels of LivedEarth-AngelParadise –*

        The Angel Stays of Memory

    O! THE A- LEAP OF TANGSTAMEMO.

    Still lifting-gifting-withing me – forward!

    O! Eternity in Time – the Staying-Song With Us as our Choir sings.

    O! Time of Resilient Earthen Paradise Anow!

It's all so overpowering!! Often, I cry loudly into this strangeness.

Eyes tear of this strangest of times, where I'm no stranger

To the Augurs of Danger, Children's laughter –

Wonder roiled by thunder and poverties of hunger.

O! Come ye tight hugs of a lover's forever,

Midst thoughts that it all could soon be over --

As such a minor statistic disappears

Into short-term memory's short-term tears.

    Eternal Sleep. Another one's magic done.

    Perhaps, in time's eternal now, a gracenote toned in tune.

    Strange Music! I'll not even know when I'm gone.

    Or hear how the symphony plays on and on and on,

    But, for now, a gracenote in the sing-along

    Choired in my own belongsong of home-tone-poetries.

Still the susta-i-nable "i" of HAPP "i" NESS in the midst of it all.

That "i" in GEN "i" US, in EX "i" ST. PR "i" DE of Life beyond GR "i" EF.

Life's RES -ili- ENT *-- AL "i" VE --* holding mindfulness with the unknowns.

O! This Stay-With-Me Embrace – of Angel's Wings Flowing --

An ultimate lifting and gracing our time's meaning of life.

It's a strange time – this life. Wonderfully --- deathly --- strange.

Ancestral Alleluia Angels fly from pages, passages, persons – Then&Now!
Their STAY-Withness of Companionship far exceeding PRAY-Worship of Otherness.
O! How I'm held by this holding-held Song of EarthAngels of Now's Evermore.
Our Stay-With-Me-Angels – lifting-inspiring, for all passages of worth.

To Have and to Hold -- Until death do us part!

In this strangeness we sing in unison – *THE HALLEHOLDON CHORUS ---*
HALLEHOLDYOU! HALLEHOLDME! HALLEHOLDWE! HALLESTAYWITHUS
(O! THE A-LEAP OF TANGSTAMEMO O O O O O!)
HALLEHOLDUS! --- HALLEHOLDON ! --- HALLELUJAH !

A NOTE OF GOTMOL'S HISTORY AND CONCLUSION

Dante's Beatrice was a real-life person before she became the angelic presence to lead him through the Paradise of his Divine Comedy. For this task, she was given sway over Virgil who guided him through both Hell and Purgatory (a pagan poet whom he knew only through his writings and history – but was, still, a guiding- Stay-With presence in Dante's real-life as such others are in ours). I consider it false to say, as some have, that Virgil ceased guidance at the gates of Heaven because he was as pre-Christian pagan. No. Such were salvageable through the rigors of Purgatory. No. Dante wanted/needed to display another Stay-With Angel, who came from his real-life experience with her. She married another and was dead at age 25, but Dante knew her enthrall of his imagination and grasp of living's truths by seeing her a few times in his life. There is no accounting of there ever being even a touch of hands or gaze into one another's eyes. He was "held" her being in "his" time and "her presence" with him. Beatrice was for Dante an "angelic-divine" presencing of The Hold that one Beholds through being Held in its Blessing.

The fact that the name Beatrice is implied within the words beatific-beatification-beatify-beatitude is obvious. They all imply "blessedness-blessings." And so it is, as I think it, that Dante "beholds" (as the beholder) in Beatrice -- that which is the Beholden experienced as Being Held. Indeed, something "everlasting." The Angelic is that which continues to "hold" (Stay-With) and "bless" – from memory's paradise or in one's current life. It is the "I-Thou" becoming an "US" – that holds us in the Held. The Beholder Beholding the Beholden to being Beheld – is not just the form/presence of persons, but of scenes, events, flowers, creatures, art: music and song, perhaps, the most universal of "holds" and "forms" everlasting. (Everlasting is an everhold – Eternity is an evertime. Their union, as in US, is The Infinite Holding Pattern that Holds us in Time.)

I'm not a Dante scholar, and make no attempt here to proof-text my interpretation. Dante is like another Virgil for me. Unlike such, as unknowns in one's real-life experiences, I've known a few "real" Beatrices and others who qualify to be likenesses of Virgil and Dante. From them, their legacies, and all who compose significant "othernesses-blessednesses" for me, I've known Paradise(s) on Earth and they Stay-With-Me. The concept of "Angels" fits for me, really-poetically-visually, to document this feature of lived experience of the "everlasting" on Planet Earth. In today's world, they are photo-images that continue and surpass their capture in the arts, dream and memory of humanity's past. Their photos and memorable representations are everywhere in "form and substance" today.

In Dante, it is as if, almost, the past and present co-exist to form a sense of eternity in time, the everlasting of our beholdings. Often, the veil lifts but momentarily as it did for Dante through Beatrice. Some sparks of enlightenment fly into consciousness…and transform comprehension. The words "form" and "transform" are dynamic to the concepts of The Hold and The Held as "sung" in GOTMOL. At the conclusion of Paradise, Dante seems much of the same mind. Here, from the last words of Canto – XXXIII, which concludes the book, this excerpt on "form":[Chartwell Books, 1982 – Rev. Francis Cary's translation.]

> O Grace, unenvying of thy boon! that gavest
> Boldness to fix so earnestly my ken
> On the everlasting splendor, that I look'd,
> While sight was unconsumed; and, in that depth,
> Saw in one volume clasp'd of love. Whatever
> The universe unfolds; all properties
> Of substance and of accident, beheld,
> Compounded, yet one individual light
> The whole. And of such bond methinks I saw
> The universal form. . . .As one,
> Who versed in geometric lore, would fain
> Measure the circle; and, though pondering long
> And deeply, that beginning, which he needs,
> Finds not: e'en such was I, intent to scan
> That novel wonder, and trace out the form,
> How to the circle fitted, and therein
> How placed: but the light was not for my wing;
> Had not a flash darted athwart my mind,
> And, in the spleen, unfolded what I sought.
> Here vigor fail'd the towering fantasy:
> But yet the will roll'd onward, like a wheel
> In even motion, by the love impell'd
> That moves the sun in heaven and all the stars.

[Angels are triune: Animus-Anima & Animate—Virgil-Beatrice & The Hold: I-Thou & an US twi-i-xt the wings! A SYNTANGOION! A Togetherness as sometimes told and felt in the "spleen" as "universal form"— as the "BEHELD, COMPOUDED…THE WHOLE" and as "The love impell'd that moves . . ." all existence to be "rolled" as it is. --- The magic of "Love," after all, is that wonderful feel of "Holding" and "Being Held." It's not living in the past, but with the Paradise of the past carried concurrently with the Paradise of now – and the persistent promise of the future. Alas, there is a reciprocity of holdings to create The Held. – It's the Stay-With & The Holdon: like two wings lifting a blessedness to grasp the apple, reach the stars -- feel blessed-caressed. O! To sing cantatas of Glorias for the Highest Holds & Loftiest Wing-Spans of this Life – *Come Home my lovely Spring – My Summer Soul has too long been Wintering. – To Have and to Hold – Until Death do Us Part.*]

APPENDIX III

O! THERE ARE TIMES

O!There are times,
I wish I were but like a dew drop
On a petal of a pansy or clover leaf
To be lifted by the glow of dawn
Into gathers of clouds, breezes, and the birded-blue of the air
Returning to Earth someday as rain --
Riding a sunbeam's warmth to fresh a garden,
Urge a dandelion in the grass,
Be some glory's gurgle in a stream where minnows play.

O! There are times,
I wish I could ink an inkling of a seedling's release,
Catch a rainbow on a casted line,
Sonnet the winged array of honking geese,
Say the perfect taste of fresh water – its splash on my face.
So much magic sparkles in this sphere of space
Spectrums of galaxies glistened in a tear.

O! Wraps of Mom's sandwiches for the school-yard lunch.
O! So brush-stroke-perfect my Love's portrait of our little dog.
O! Dad's hold of his tremored hands to steady-paint a name on a truck.
O! Children's clinging laughter on the spin of the Merry-Go-Round.
O! My breath's breathlessness as some beauty lifts its hands to my face.

O! There are times,
I think I've been held by what holds – the home in the poem --
Like dew on the pansy petal or the clover leaf,
Sailing astraddle dawn's awakening dolphin lift,
Feeling aroused to thrive alive again in the held of the hold:
Stroll the garden holding hands, kissing flowers-- tastes of dew --
With thoughts of you and you and you . . . . . .
Those whens of when never to happen again.
There are times – ever more the more to any one's story--
Of loves lost -- into stays that hold – keeping time with memory.

O! I know love's labor must ever-work this garden's every dream –
Tasking transformation's ride-the-tides of sunbeams ever new.
O! This mote of dust held in the universe of a drop of dew.
Life in Death-Death in Life – Life on each end of the stream.

O! The waiting till it's time
To be lifted within that grasp of morning's dawn.
Each will be present – as must be . . . for what can't go on.
Such are times of always – snowflakes dancing in the sun --
As all "livings" are released from their hold
As some new Spring breaks through the cold,
With seedlings longing for newer rain;
Held 'til some "become" comes home again
With growing's burst from the dark by the break of day:
A Fireflies At Dawn Poiesis – poetries still untold --
To grasp what hugs in the held -- ever greater light to behold.

O! There are times. . .
Likes of thee and me, holding-notes to their pitch;
Brevity's voice -- waiting some eternity's pinch
To statistic a quotidian toll of another step-in-time.
O! The end times' rime – for which all are due –
Balancing harmonies with complexities --
As clocks fall off the wall for pall after pall of me and you.

O! To wish one's mote be gently held as by a drop of dew:
Some note of collective calm grasped in a tune or two,
A gracenote – gleaned as blissful gracings from glistens of dawn,
As time's bow plays across the lairs and grasses of the lawn --
Rising a chorus to sing, on-time-in-tune with each light of day;
Lifted serene as aspires of joy – where nature and art share time's lay --
Icicles' dropping-ping tuned with great cathedral gongings:
EarthAngels called to gather memory's choir. . .
That harmony of clouds, breezes, the birded-blue of the air:
Some glory's gurgle gracing a stream where minnows play!
O! There are times… .
So many "only-OUR-omnipresent" times

Of..........oooooOOOO.................!!!

MDOK--1/28/21 [With "nudges" from Yeat's *Byzantium* poems and today's doomsday clock of climate crises and mutant pandemics. Humanity and Earth are in a wrestle of hugs that hold-true and have-nots to release as never before. Such are the times for the Philosopher's Stone to roll with Science and Nobility, and Poetries to Awaken with Daylight and the Holding Of Hands throughout the voicings of the choir.]

O ! THE MOM ZIE KAI OF GOTMOL !

ABOUT THE AUTHOR

Born 2/18/34. I left my (blue-collar) home at 18 with $125 from paper route and Kroger's carry-out-boy tips. On my own ever-since. Worked through a BA Degree - 1956 (English/Theater) at WVU. Drafted into the Army. A Cryptographer at SHAPE in Fountainebleau, France. Then telephone company management for four years. Married Marilyn in 1960 (Children born 1961, 1965, 1968: lost her to leukemia/cancer in 2009). Studied at University of Chicago/Meadville Lombard for a M.Div. Degree in 1966. Later, 1976, an M.A. Degree in Clinical Psychology from Ball State University. I'm a colon-cancer survivor – age 50 Antibiotics put me in hearing aids forever. Survived heart-attack at 76. (Various surgeries-procedures from age 10 to date. COPD since 2004.) A Unitarian Universalist Minister for 30 years – 5 ministries/3 Interims. Officially retired (50th year celebration) in 2016. Always a humanistic liberal progressive spirituality with a poetic/theatric hold. (I've a second resume of Acting/Theater experience.) Chaplain with the Long Beach, CA Police Department for over three years. Back in WV, became a Family Therapist for six years and UU Consulting Minister for five years. Started collecting my writings in 2005 with hopes of publication. I've not sought traditional publishing. GOTMOL is my 8th self—published book. (Self-publishing so I'd live to hold my books in hand. I'm holding better than expected.) I've no accolades or prizes from any sector. No Editors/Creators other than me. Plan to publish my children's stories in 2021. Then an APE --- Autobiographical Poetic Essay -- from my research on "consciousness." I live alone in my hillside home in WV. Three children close-by. I've sung in five different choirs in my lifetime. Wrote first poem in high school. My gracenote is still holding its play in the greater symphony. My candle's still holding in the wind. Who knows what tomorrow sings or brings! -- Along the way, my "mdok " – still belongsongs its ***Manifest Destiny's Odyssean Kairos***—as an 'Apo'kstrophes' of the Syntangoion and as a living "luminary" of the SHOALS OF WONSUNODI – ever uplifted and carried-onward by the Stay-With Angelics (those presences of lived Paradise on Earth) from my own-real-time-life. My website about the ANSWER (A New Spirituality We R) is <u>mdokelly.com.</u> I'll get my second COVID shot on 2/2/2021.

EARTHANGEL

Printed in the United States
by Baker & Taylor Publisher Services